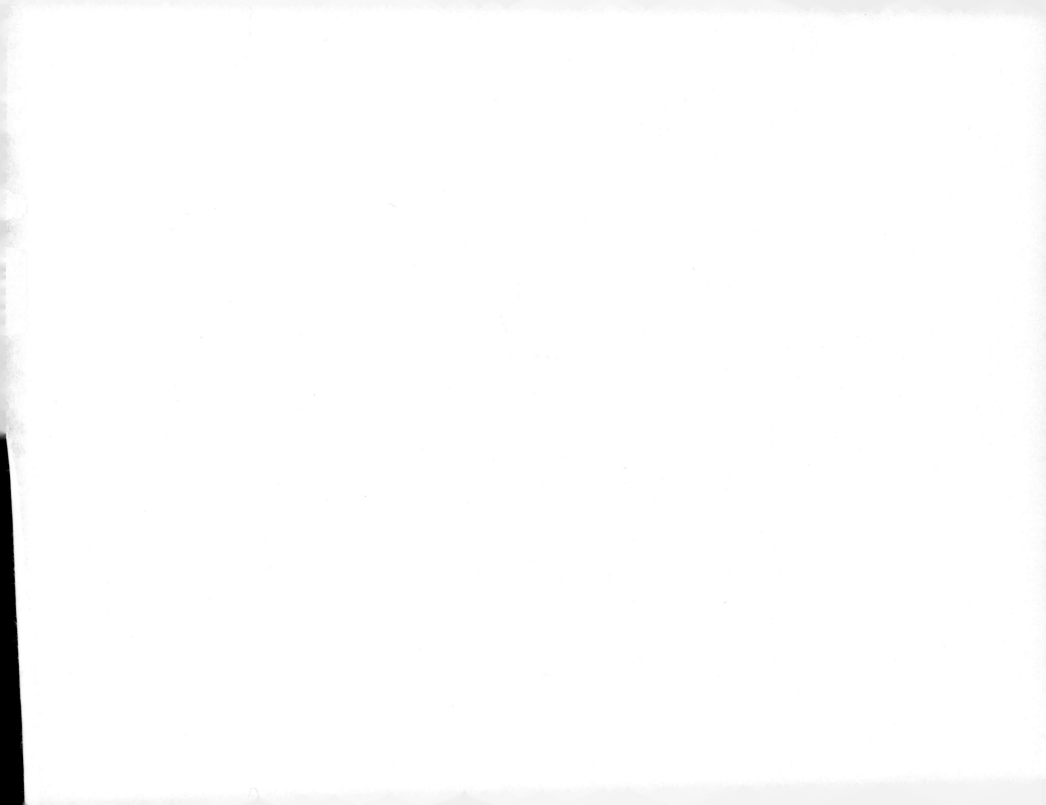

FENWAY SAVED

BILL NOWLIN & MIKE ROSS
WITH JIM PRIME

Photography by Mike Ross

SPORTS PUBLISHING INC.

www.SportsPublishingInc.com

A **SPORTS**MASTERS Book

ISBN 1-58382-020-5
Library of Congress Catalog Card Number: 99-62432

SPORTS PUBLISHING INC.

www.SportsPublishingInc.com
A **SPORTS**MASTERS Book

Editor, Director of Production: Tom Bast
Interior Design and Layout: Scot Muncaster
Dustjacket Design: Scot Muncaster

Front Cover Photography: Peter Travers
Back Cover Photography: Mike Ross

Printed in the United States.

The publisher gratefully acknowledges use of quoted material from the following sources:

2. A BRIEF HISTORY OF FENWAY PARK
Gershman, Michael, DIAMONDS (Boston & New York: Houghton Mifflin, 1993)
Williams, Ted, MY TURN AT BAT (NY: Simon & Schuster, 1969)

3. THE WALL
Chadwick, Bruce & David M. Spindel, THE BOSTON RED SOX (NY: Abbeville, 1992)
DiMaggio, Dom with Bill Gilbert, REAL GRASS, REAL HEROES (New York: Zebra Books, 1990)
Gershman, Michael, DIAMONDS (Boston & New York: Houghton Mifflin, 1993)
Higgins, George V., THE PROGRESS OF THE SEASONS (New York: Prentice-Hall, 1989)
Hirshberg, Al, THE RED SOX, THE BEAN, AND THE COD (Boston: Waverly House, 1947)
Hirshberg, Al, WHAT'S THE MATTER WITH THE RED SOX? (New York: Dodd, Mead & Company, 1973)
Hough, John, Jr., A PLAYER FOR A MOMENT (New York: Harcourt, Brace, Jovanovich, 1988)
Lee, Bill "Spaceman" with Dick Lally, THE WRONG STUFF (NY: Penguin, 1985)
Mann, Jack, "The Great Wall of Boston," SPORTS ILLUSTRATED, June 28, 1965
Nolan, Martin, in Riley, Dan (ed.), THE RED SOX READER (Thousand Oaks, Ca.: Ventura Arts, 1987)
Sullivan, George, THE PICTURE HISTORY OF THE BOSTON RED SOX (Indianapolis & New York: Bobbs Merrill, 1979)
Thorn, John & Pete Palmer, THE HIDDEN GAME OF BASEBALL (Garden City, LI, NY: Doubleday, 1985)
Yastrzemski, Carl and Gerald Eskenazi, YAZ: BASEBALL, THE WALL AND ME (New York: Doubleday, 1990)

4. THE GROUNDS
For Epigram: Machen, Arthur, in Secker, Martin, THE ART OF WANDERING (London: Village Press, 1924)
Bryan, Mike, BASEBALL LIVES (NY: Pantheon, 1989)
Clark, Ellery, BOSTON RED SOX (Hicksville LI NY: Exposition Press, 1975)
Feller, Sherm, FOREVER FENWAY (video)
Higgins, George, op. cit.
Johnson, Dick & Glenn Stout, TED WILLIAMS: A PORTRAIT IN WORDS AND PICTURES (New York: Walker and Company, 1991)
Levin, Ted, "A Bird Watcher's Guide to Fenway Park," YANKEE magazine, May 1993
Smith, Curt, VOICES OF THE GAME (NY: Firestone, 1992)
Sullivan, George, THE PICTURE HISTORY OF THE BOSTON RED SOX (Indianapolis & New York: Bobbs Merrill, 1979)
Yastrzemski, Carl and Gerald Eskenazi, YAZ: BASEBALL, THE WALL AND ME (New York: Doubleday, 1990)

5. AROUND THE PARK
Angell, Roger, THE SUMMER GAME (NY: Popular Library, 1978)
Arnold, Eric, A DAY IN THE LIFE OF A BASEBALL PLAYER - MO VAUGHN (New York: Scholastic, 1996.)
Cataneo, David, PEANUTS AND CRACKERJACK (Nashville: Rutledge Hill Press, 1991)
DiMaggio, Dom with Bill Gilbert, REAL GRASS, REAL HEROES (New York: Zebra Books, 1990)
Falkner, David, NINE SIDES OF THE DIAMOND (NY: Firestone, 1990)
Higgins, George V., THE PROGRESS OF THE SEASONS (New York: Prentice-Hall, 1989)
Hough, John, Jr., A PLAYER FOR A MOMENT (New York: Harcourt, Brace, Jovanovich, 1988)
Isaacs, Neil, INNOCENCE AND WONDER (Indianapolis: Masters Press, 1994)
Kinsella, W. P., SHOELESS JOE (NY: Ballantine Books, 1983)
Lee, Bill "Spaceman" with Dick Lally, THE WRONG STUFF (NY: Penguin, 1985)
Smith, Curt, op. cit.
Stanley, Bob in Riley, Dan (ed.), THE RED SOX READER (Thousand Oaks, Ca.: Ventura Arts, 1987)
Sullivan, George, THE PICTURE HISTORY OF THE BOSTON RED SOX (Indianapolis & New York: Bobbs Merrill, 1979)
Updike, John in Riley, Dan (ed.), THE RED SOX READER (Thousand Oaks, Ca.: Ventura Arts, 1987)
Yastrzemski, Carl and Gerald Eskenazi, YAZ: BASEBALL, THE WALL AND ME (New York: Doubleday, 1990)

6. FENWAY PARK AND THE AMERICAN CULTURAL LANDSCAPE
Bronski, Matthew Bolster, "The Garden in the Machine: The Cultural Landscape of the Urban Major League Baseball Parks of 1909-1923," University of Pennsylvania Master's Thesis, 1995. This section owes a great debt to Bronski's thesis, and many of the ideas and quotations herein are borrowed from Bronski's work.
Cowan, Michael H., CITY OF THE WEST: EMERSON, AMERICA AND URBAN METAPHOR (New Haven: Yale University Press, 1967)
Gershman, DIAMONDS (op. cit.)
Giamatti, A. Bartlett, "A Ballpark is Freedom's Ring" A LIFE OF A. BARTLETT GIAMATTI by Anthony Valerio
Goodwin, Doris Kearns, "From Father with Love" in "Literati on the Red Sox," Boston Globe, 6 October 1986, special section.
Marx, Leo, THE MACHINE IN THE GARDEN (New York, Oxford University Press, 1964)
Mumford, Lewis, "The Megamachine - I," THE NEW YORKER, 10 October 1970
Nolan, Martin, "From Frazee to Fisk" in THE RED SOX READER, ed. Dan Riley.
Patton, Phil, "The Wall, and Other Bizarre Afflictions Pertaining to Boston's Crypto-Mythical Red Sox," CONNOISSEUR, September 1986

DEDICATION

To my mother who took me to Fenway Park for the first time and to my daughter to whom I passed on the favor.

— Mike Ross

To my father Bill Sr., who first brought me to Fenway; my wife Yleana, who indulges my frequent visits; my son Emmet, who's in part being brought up there (and got his first foul ball from the bat boy in 1998); and to my partners at Rounder Records.

— Bill Nowlin

TABLE OF CONTENTS

ACKNOWLEDGMENTS

I began photographing Fenway Park in the early summer of 1982 on a day when the New England sunshine revealed the park in its rarified glory. Over the next few years, with fine weather and a following wind, I accumulated around 200 worthy images snapped through 1990, just after the Red Sox added the 600 Club and shunted the press box into the stratosphere.

In my mind's eye I had imagined a well produced book of handsome images, with choice words and exquisite quotes. Then along came Bill Nowlin who said, at once, that he wished to join me. Bill provided the motor and compass, and contributed unimagined avenues of endeavor. He and Jim Prime had recently produced *Ted Williams: A Tribute* so, with Jim Prime's involvement, *Fenway Saved* was blessed with a fine writer and editor, a real pro with a good eye for detail. Jim provided vital ballast during our headlong journey.

I owe my inspiration to Fenway, and to the master-writers and poets such as Roger Angell, Bart Giamatti, Donald Hall, John Updike and those several others who loved Fenway Park and who extracted the finest imagery the great house had to offer, and transposed that imagery into the sacred texts of baseball.

Also I give thanks to my British hosts who took me in, gave me shelter and allowed me to conduct baseball enterprises from within their Kingdom.

— Mike Ross

Fenway Park certainly appeals to people far and wide, and this book is indicative of that. The book was created by three people, from three different countries. Mike Ross was born and raised in Portland, Maine, but has made his home in London, England, for over 35 years. Mike did the principal photography on which *Fenway Saved* is based, and offered the perspective of a talented artist to the text. I'm from Cambridge, Massachusetts. When I saw Mike's photographs and became enthused about creating the book, I talked with Tom Bast of Sports Publishing Inc.

We might have done yet another book showing scenes at the park—baseball being played, the obligatory shots of fans in the park, shots of vendors and the like. We wanted, instead, to focus on Fenway Park itself. Tom agreed to publish the book and Mike and I plunged into gathering material and writing.

Jim Prime, of New Minas, Nova Scotia, in Canada, collaborated throughout and did most of the pre-editing. He also contributed a fine Introduction. Jim and I worked together on *Ted Williams: A Tribute*, and I was really glad to work again with him once more. Most of the book was written by sharing thoughts, impressions and drafts on e-mail—a tri-national production, completed start to finish in sixty or seventy days, save for Mike's original photography.

— Bill Nowlin

The authors want to thank several people for their help in making *Fenway Saved* a reality…

Enzo Apicella, Philip Bess, Lester Bookbinder, Bob Bluthardt, Dick Bresciani, Matthew Bronski, Ted Brooks, Larry Cancro, Nancy Davidson, Mike DeSantis, Lib Dooley, Edgeware Road Photo Centre (London, England), John Eichler, Roger Errabey, Mark Fischer, Gil Galvin, John Gaustad, Bob George, Jeff Harris, Chris Heneghan, Martin Hoerchner, Henry Horenstein, Larry Hoskin, Jane Hughson, Ken Irwin, Mike Janedy, Dick Johnson, Brian Knight, Linda Kohn, Kim Konrad, Caroline Krause, Kris Krause, Bill Lee, June Levy, Robert Maas, Elliott J. Mahler, Debbie Matson, Richard Merkin, Pat Moscaritolo, Tim Naehring, Steve Netksy, Webb Nichols, William Nowlin, Sr., Lisa Olden, John Pastier, Johnny Pesky, Anne Quinn, Doug Rotondi, Tim Samway, Aaron Schmidt, Jim Schneider, June Schwartz, James Shanahan, Richmond Sheppard, Marty St. George, Society for American Baseball Research (SABR), Rocky Stone, Judy Sturwold, Superchrome (London England), Supercolour (London, England), Tom Taton, Benjamin Thompson, Jane Thompson, Maryanne Thompson, The Travel Shop, Peter Travers, Mike "The Hat" Trott, Bob Walsh, Gary Williams, Dan Wilson, John Lincoln Wright,

…and to the princes of Maine, Kings of New England.

In this book, we have standardized the capitalization of The Wall. We have done this both in our own text and in quotations from others.

FENWAY
SAVED

DISCOVERING FENWAY PARK

by Jim Prime

I first discovered Fenway Park on my radio late one spring evening in 1961 as I was nestled in bed at my home on an isolated island off the coast of Nova Scotia. Outside in the darkness, a fierce Nor'easter howled off the Bay of Fundy and a hard rain assaulted the windows of my corner bedroom. I was twelve years old.

As isolated as my island was, it ironically afforded easy access to the popular culture of the northeastern United States—New York, Philadelphia, and Boston—through the medium of radio. At night, the fickle ionosphere usually relented, allowing radio signals to skip across the open sea from Boston to my trusty Philco 12–transistor. It was in this manner, then, that announcers Curt Gowdy and Ned Martin introduced me to Fenway Park. Only later, well after my initiation into this other world, was I to discover that many area fishermen would regularly tune in to Red Sox games while hauling their lines.

Throughout this game, and in the hundreds I listened to subsequently, Gowdy and Martin made casual, but repeated references to the Green Monster—a.k.a. The Wall (not to be confused with the Monster, a.k.a. reliever Dick Radatz, who entered the scene the following year). They also spoke matter-of-factly about the unique dimensions, about every angle and gap that distinguishes this ballpark from all others. To a child, the terms sounded mysterious, exciting, even slightly exotic, like some kind of incantation designed to initiate the listener into a secret society. What kind of place was this Fenway Park? It would take, I decided, nothing less than baseball's version of Camelot to live up to my lofty expectations.

Over the years, I saw a few photos of Fenway in the Red Sox yearbooks I would send away for, or occasionally some flickering black and white images on a TV Game of the Week, but the radio images remained the strongest. Through the medium of radio and the miracle of imagination, even a blind man could appreciate the beauty of Fenway Park.

Playing baseball on the island, I pretended I was stepping to the plate in Fenway, or tracking down a long fly ball in front of the right field bleachers. Our rocky, often fog-shrouded field made this a challenge to even the most fertile imagination. Located on a high bluff, it offered a breathtaking view of the Bay of Fundy on one side and St. Mary's Bay on the other, but instead of the Citgo sign beyond left field, a lighthouse flashed its warnings from atop

a sheer cliff on nearby Brier Island. Alder bushes flanked the right field foul lines, and instead of The Wall in left, there was an electric fence, beyond which grazed contented, but totally indifferent cows. The backstop had been improvised from an old fishing net, and when holes appeared, our catcher's mother served as our own "designated knitter."

Our field of dreams may have been a sort of Bizarro Fenway, but one part of it was as real as the Splendid Splinter himself: the baseballs. In the early sixties we had no money for new balls and consequently the ones we used had been taped and re–taped countless times. On a dare from the lone Yankee fan on our team (perhaps in all of Digby County), I wrote a letter to Red Sox owner Tom Yawkey asking if it would be possible to get some batting practice balls for use by our rag-tag Freeport Schooners team. Two weeks later, to my astonishment and delight, a dozen gleaming American League balls arrived at the local Canada Customs office. Some sported green stains from Fenway grass or The Wall itself, others traces of reddish infield clay. Curiously, one even carried the autograph of Minnesota Twins slugger Harmon Killebrew. I confess that I can still recall the smell of those balls, an aroma redolent of major league baseball, my beloved Red Sox, and Fenway Park. After a brief internal debate, I opted to share my wealth with the team rather than squirrel them away in my sock drawer. It not only increased my status with my teammates, but I think we played much better baseball after that. This cross-border free trade between me and Fenway

Park was repeated for the next five years.

Twenty-odd years would pass before I stepped from the grime and bustle of Lansdowne Street and entered the oasis of verdant greens and exquisite lines that decades earlier I had begun constructing in my mind's eye. To me the experience was like meeting someone you had previously known only known as a pen pal and finding them exactly as you had expected them to be. Lines from the classic John Updike article on Ted Williams' last game came to mind: "Fenway Park, in Boston, is a lyric little bandbox of a ballpark. Everything is painted green and seems in curiously sharp focus, like the inside of an old-fashioned peeping-type Easter egg."

Fenway is frequently described as angular, but I quickly discovered that it is also avuncular. Visiting Fenway is like dropping in on a favorite eccentric uncle, the one your parents like but don't quite approve of. The uncle who lives alone, save for too many cats, and tells overly graphic stories of war and slightly salacious tales of love to impressionable nieces and nephews. The one who after the third whiskey and soda rolls up his pant leg and proudly shows where he was

wounded by sniper fire while storming the beaches of Dieppe. The one whose attic is a fascinating place full of dusty nick-nacks and artifacts of bygone days. At once disheveled and immaculate, alternately a self-deprecating gentleman and a cigar-chomping braggart, this uncle has an infectious good will. Fenway Park is as unconventional as Uncle Fester, as unpretentious as Uncle Buck, and as American as Uncle Sam.

I entered the park with trepidation, fearing the reality could never live up to the holy of holies I had first created in my boundless, youthful imagination. I looked around to confirm that all was as it should be: The Wall, which thrusts itself at right-handed hitters like a buxom showgirl enticing some rube just in from the sticks; the manually operated scoreboard; the deep right field angling sharply to the shallow foul pole; the lone red seat, in a vast sea of green seats, deep in the right field stands, marking the spot where

Ted Williams' perfect swing had once deposited a baseball. Everything was as my radio tour guides described it, and I looked respectfully up to the acropolis from which they had imparted their wisdom. Even the New England atmosphere—as thick as any Nova Scotia fog—had been preordained by Martin and Gowdy. The hot dog vendors with their distinctive Boston accents, the ushers with their casual certitude, the demeanor of the crowd—the most knowledgeable fans in baseball—for who else would be worthy to worship in such a shrine?—were all just as they should be. Even the degree of cynicism they exhibited didn't shock me, for I knew well the Red Sox history, the disappointments and the drought of World Series championships.

When I first discovered Fenway, the Red Sox were a weak team, an also-ran. Williams had exited with one of the most dramatic home runs in history, and Yaz had just entered, stage left, to join an unimpressive supporting cast. Perhaps that's why the park itself held such importance for me; it was always at its peak; it never had a bad day, never disappointed. The players were actors on a very special stage. Shakespeare claimed that the play's the thing but when Williams or Yaz made a play off the left field wall, the Green Monster always got equal billing from the announcer. All great stages are like that. Carnegie Hall is as famous as anyone who performed there. So are the Grand Ole Opry, and the Old Vic. Perhaps in Shakespearean times, the Globe Theater's appeal was equal to that of its actors.

Fenway has had its own Macbeths and Othellos

and Hamlets and even the occasional Falstaff. Tragic heroes abound, even Greco-Roman ones: the Greek Harry Agganis and the Italian Tony Conigliaro, both sons of New England and both struck down in their prime. Ruth (who seemed unsure if he was playing Falstaff, Hamlet, or both simultaneously) performed there, so did Foxx, Ted, Yaz, Clemens, Mo and Nomar. Comic relief has been provided by Pumpsie Green and Gene Conley and Spaceman Lee and El Tiante and the puckish Dick (Dr. Strangeglove) Stuart. They all left their imprint on the place, some literally—Williamsburg, Conig's Corner, Pesky's Pole—some numerically—9,4,1,8—(the retired numbers of Ted, Joe Cronin, Bobby Doerr and Yaz)—and added to the lore. There are many ghosts in Fenway Park—friendly ghosts for the most part, but fearful apparitions as well, since the spectres of Casper-like Bucky Dent and a limping Bill Buckner, the Ghost of Big Miss Past still disturb the sleep of Bosox fans.

At almost the same time I began listening to games from Fenway, I had discovered Yankee Stadium on my radio, but the image was not nearly as rich or defined or lasting. The Yankees were a juggernaut, and the team commanded my attention, but not Yankee Stadium. If this place was avuncular, it was only in the sense of the overachieving uncle who tousled your hair, and offered stock tips, but couldn't quite remember your name. Yankee Stadium may have been billed as the house that Ruth built, but the Bambino apprenticed at Fenway before he built it.

Fenway's origins were never so grand; it was not built by one man but by hundreds of long forgotten immigrant workmen. Its reputation began with the first game played there, and it is still under construction. The reputation's foundation was laid by the likes of Ruth and Hooper and Lewis and Smokey Joe Wood; the frame was raised by the next shift, forged to steely permanence by names such as Foxx and Williams and Doerr and Yaz. And each time Nomar or another new Red Sox hero steps to the plate and hits a home run over The Wall, he further reinforces that reputation.

Mike Ross, the versatile artist whose photographs adorn this book, sees beauty and worth in every nook and corner of Fenway, and views the ballpark as an architectural and artistic masterpiece. Nonetheless, even man's great works must often bow to the inevitable, sometimes to be replaced by newer things; occasionally by better things. Whether life imitates art or vice versa, both are transitory. Other cultural icons have come and gone: Ebbets Field and the Polo Grounds are no more. Venerable Montreal Forum, which at times seemed to house the dreams and aspirations of all Quebecois, has succumbed to the wrecker's ball. So has Boston Garden and Maple Leaf Gardens. Each time another of these landmarks disappears, it increases the symbolic value of Fenway as bridge to the past.

Sadly, commercial interests dictate that one day Fenway may be little more than a fond memory, a gentle remembrance first passed in hushed tones from father to son, and then reverentially from grand-father to grandson, until eventually it transcends the realm of baseball and becomes part of the rich mosaic of our past. Fenway will then be saved, and will continue to beckon us back to a time and a place when mortal gods played out our dreams on emerald fields. Fenway Park is the home field for a chosen few major leaguers who were able to make their dreams come true, but more importantly, it is the repository for a million adolescent fantasies and as many piercing, bittersweet memories. As such, the spirit of Fenway will live on as long as such dreams remain a part of the human condition.

We depend really on Ken Coleman and Joe Castiglione—the radio game with its background noises of vendors and heckling, rise and swoop of public hope and despair. Regular listeners learn to decode the announcer's pitch-pattern, so that when bat-crack meets the crowd-roar Ken Coleman's first words—"Buckner hits a long…"—tell me single, long out or possible home run long before his words announce it.

[Ken Coleman] broadcast 31 seasons of major league baseball with a soft attentiveness and the gentlest irony in the Eastern United States. He's not given to false enthusiasm, artificial excitement or gross charm. He's literate, friendly and dependable; you trust the man, and that's how we want it.

– Donald Hall

YANKEES
RANDOLPH   2B
GRIFFEY   CF
WINFIELD   LF
PINIELLA   RF
HOBSON   →DH
NETTLES   3B
WYNEGAR   C
COLLINS   1B
DENT   SS

MAGNAVOX

360

Baseball's Masterpiece

by Mike Ross

It has acquired character. It's weathered, it's tattered and torn, with paint painted over old paint, but the layers and lines only add to its value and charm. Fenway is where the artist's palette and the sculptor's clay met the designer's drawing board to create a rare piece of architecture and a work of art unlike any other on the North American landscape. But it's also a work of art in which one can actually walk around, thus becoming part of this *tableau vivant* for a few precious hours.

If Wrigley Field is about bricks and ivy, Fenway Park is primarily about contour and color, the predominant color being a sort of smoky green, a green which has changed little over the decades. Some would argue that the green is a cobalt green, while others might insist that it is *terre verte* mixed with viridian. On certain hot August summer days, you'd swear that a dash of raw sienna or Indian yellow had been added to the mix. At those times, you can imagine Paul Gauguin and Vincent Van Gogh down on the concourse arguing the fine points of raw sienna versus new gamboge.

I like the idea that no one has tried to alter the state of the park's primary appearance, yet I love the notion of the ballpark subtly changing its mood from game to game, depending on the light. The precise colors are a mystery, possibly ground to a powder from ancient pigments into a secret formula. Whatever its derivation or formulation, it is a green more distinctive, and more representative of English-Irish Boston, than the shamrocks sported by those crosstown sons of Erin, the basketball Celtics. Even the grass has a special richness of greens. Has a diamond ever appeared so emerald? Yet the outfield turf shows a tinge of blue—Kentucky bluegrass, durable and handsome, complementing Fenway's painted fences.

It's really quite astonishing that Fenway has evolved over 65 years since its last major renovation, and still managed to maintain such aesthetic consistency. The reasons may be manifold, but it is a fair guess that when Tom and Jean Yawkey approved the design and decor of their cherished bit of real estate, they issued a decree guaranteeing, in trust, the stability and longevity of what ultimately was to be recognized as an architectural gem.

The young couple presciently chose design and colors that formed an alliance of forthright geometry with the strong tones inherent in the Art Deco movement of the early 20th Century. Along with the accompanying Oriental and Egyptian flavors, the colors were a deep blue (lapis lazuli), cherry red, and of course the de rigeur lighter *eau-de Nil*, a pale green tinged

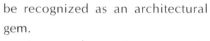

4

with a hint of the muddy River Nile. These colors can be spotted at various locations in the park, the green being the absolute star color of the concourse beneath the stands, and probably also the color of the outfield walls before they were slightly darkened.

The conservators of Fenway seem to be on full-time duty. They, whoever they are, have done their part in preserving the integrity and constancy of the place. The red paint on the earlier cast iron seats is not a "hot" red like the team uniform trim. It is a lacquer red, a cherry red. I imagine that way back in time, when the park was given its first coat, the refined first lady of Boston baseball, Jean Yawkey, exclaimed that the red on the uniforms was "too

garish for this ballpark," perhaps removing from her pocket book a red lacquered Japanese compact case of carved and polished wood obtained on a recent voyage to the East. "Let's paint it like this, Tom!" she might well have intoned in her cultivated way. The navy trim on the same seats, though a dark navy, radiates richness, the deepness of tone giving way to a hint of ultramarine and a touch of Prussian blue.

In keeping with the lacquer red and eau-de-Nil green, Fenway also sports Oriental and exotic overtones that would score perfect marks in the eyes of a *feng shui* master. "It's comfortable, it's chummy," as Speaker of the U.S. House (and Fenway habitué) Tip O'Neill opined, "It's like being in your own home." And if fans are comfortable in their own homes then they will feel at home in Fenway Park even if they know nothing about the art of feng shui.

The Park itself is captivating. In a domain where the Cabots will speak only to the Lowells, how ironic that a city such as Boston, Puritan and standoffish within the perception of American culture and the ethos of the city's founding fathers, allows such a democratic, less conservative proximity of fans to the playing field. Such an intimacy is yet another wonderful facet of the gem.

If you look around Fenway, you'll see that it's wrapped tight, like a gift, with no loose ends. The wrapping extends around The Wall, around each corner lovingly folded and trimmed, each outfield panel, each door

leading onto the field, the bullpen fence, the camera pits and the cable conduits. Was that idea borrowed from the great artist Christo? Starting in 1958, Christo began small by wrapping domestic and industrial artifacts, eventually tying up 1.5 miles of Australian coastline (with one quarter million feet of fabric), and then wrapping the Reichstag in Berlin. He recently wrapped up the trees in a French orchard for the winter exhibiting, as does Fenway, a tenderness toward nature. Red Sox groundskeeper Mr. Mooney would almost certainly smile at such nonfunctional efforts as wrapping the Pont Neuf in Paris; yet he, too, lovingly wraps nature: the outfield grass at Fenway Park is covered with white felt each winter, to protect it from the ice.

Around the outside facing the street are the subtle diamond motifs of the brickwork, period green capitols in concrete relief, and a bronze plaque honoring Thomas A. Yawkey with its American League eagle symbol, possibly influenced by the Pectoral of Ramses II (XIX dynasty). Indeed, Fenway recalls architectural influences of ancient temples and holy missions, from the Temple of Horus, 200 BC, to the Mission of St. Francis of Assisi at Mission Ranchos de Taos, New Mexico. Frank Lloyd Wright gathered all those influences into his early 20th Century temples, and his works may well

9

"It is clear that all modern masterpieces have some archetypal idea behind them."
– Charles Jenks, The Independent

have suggested the existing angles and contours of Fenway Park to the reputable Cleveland architects at Osborn Engineering who designed the original 1912 version of the park and subsequently prescribed the changes during the Yawkey days.

Fenway survives as a temple of baseball, a cathedral of greens built over the decades, yet its style never departing from the original vision, any more than did the Milan Cathedral, which took almost 500 years to complete. Fenway has stood up to multiple alterations, becoming more gorgeous and more appreciated. From the replacement of the wooden outfield stands by the great sculptural concrete bleachers to the joining of the bullpens onto the right field stands, these alterations added to the wonder and the increasing complexity of the park. It got older, but it got better.

Fenway has an almost magical ability to uplift and transform. Is it the thrilling yet soothing lines and contours that lift the spirit and fortify the soul? Notice how the left field grandstand rises up to join The Wall, giving further rise to the golden yellow foul line and foul pole. The configuration of the center field walls and bleachers, and the bullpen and right field bleachers lock together into a perfect juxtaposing of obtuse triangles, rectangles, trapezoids, and squares in a three dimensional, Euclid-

ean crazy-quilt. Roger Angell best described the daring and bulky contours and obtuse angles of Fenway as the "ultimate origami."

This is architecture, and it is sculpture and design and color, and it is beautiful. As a piece of architecture, the park is quite indescribable in the technical language used by practitioners of the trade. Fenway is an aberration. Consider its monstrously surreal Wall. It extends from left field almost to dead center. Walls of such stature have been built in the past to keep out the marauding Vandals. The painter Breughel in his "Tower of Babel" might have been charged with creating such a folly. From the beginning, the park would have to live with the fact that it was weird, weird in the sense that it is, overall, of odd and inexplicable character. This definition would suffice to describe the fate of the team that has played there, intrinsically and symbiotically bound, as one, with its surroundings. This coinci-

315
96

dence of team and surroundings gave birth to a history so rich with strange tales, that it reads like a piece of fiction, with the density of an Icelandic saga.

Subsequent alterations carried out at Fenway Park would only be done under the watchful eye of The Wall itself, which fiercely guards its power. That power extends to more than just its architectural design. It gives with one hand and takes away with the other. It is an infuriating master which, dictated by the confinement created by Landsdowne Street below it—as if endowed with a mind of its own—thrives on its role in the divine comedy that has been played out within the construct of Fenway Park, thus creating exciting theater in keeping with the nature of its surroundings. (Divine it may be, but if only we fans could forget the pain, and figure out where in the hell the comedy is supposed to be.)

The sweep of the lines: one comes back to it again and again. The center field bleachers, how they rise up narrowing at the top, crowned now by an awesome black scoreboard, then swooping

down, headlong, on a geometric mission to their right field counterparts. Then add to the solid geometry the shadows which they create, thereby multiplying, compounding, and augmenting the equation, adding even more surfaces and facets for the eyes to dwell upon. The sun comes into the picture and all at once an everyday trapezoid is transformed into an irregular pentagon.

Our eyes at times are unable to determine where the architecture ends and the shadows begin. Indeed, as the season shifts, you never know which Fenway you'll get. The perfect consistency of sharp angles created by the sun also affects the indoors with piercing shafts of light penetrating the dusky interior, softly settling on the concrete floor, glancing off pillars and walls, gently gracing the souvenir stands and glorifying the interior greenness.

The painters of the 1920s, Fenninger and Sheeler come to mind, as does Edward Hopper, explored those shafts of light in their works. Unknown to the Red Sox, their ballpark had become an oil painting. The ceiling area is another throw-away sculptural wonder, a concrete logjam of crisscrossing beams similar to the architectural illusions of one M.C. Escher. All this unbeknownst to the reveling crowd below, who nonetheless are graciously affected.

Further along the irregular construct, the bleachers in right stretch back and up, looming over the Williamsburg bullpens in right, adding further magnificence found in no other American sporting arena. Williamsburg was built onto the front of the right

field seats, thus shortening the home run distance for young Ted Williams, while helping to define the strangest center field configuration in baseball—an outfielder's nightmare in which he may have to literally turn a corner to make a catch at the 420-foot mark. Red Sox and visiting pitchers warm up in these grandiose bullpens, not at long distance, as in Yankee Stadium, hidden from the fans, but previewing their stuff directly to the fans. The bullpens are an integral part of the schematic, unlike other ballparks. The pitcher warms up in the way a pitcher should—in full view of a

mass of critics, some friendly. No other sport offers such intimacy with the spectators. Baseball has always been rather gracious that way, and Boston has been the most gracious of all.

Look at how close the on-deck circle is to fans. Teddy Ballgame could confirm that it is almost spitting distance; so close you can tell if The Kid forgot to shave today or if Babe Ruth, betrayed by bloodshot eyes, made it home only a few hours after curfew last night.

Fenway Saved

In Fenway, anywhere you choose to point a camera produces a good shot. The park is photogenic, verging on spectacular from every viewpoint—through a long lens, wide or regular, 22mm, 35mm, 135mm, 1.2, 3.5, open wide, or shut to a pin point; you needn't be an expert to capture the allúre of Fenway. Just read the light, focus and, voila!, you're a regular Picasso.

We think of Fenway in terms of character and personality, the odd angles and crazy tangents, the excitement guaranteed by those daring lines, evolved over the decades from the simplest of New England designs. Indeed the beauty of the place lies in its very simplicity and the utility of its design. What we have is the most aesthetically pleasing of all ballparks, perhaps because of all the ballparks, Fenway is the only one that has been left to evolve from its origins, rather than deny them.

Over the decades, Fenway Park, like no other sporting domain, has remained true to itself and to the New

Baseball's Masterpiece

Wrigley Field would appear as having a grand concourse.

If you get off at the "Fenway Park" subway stop, you are not at the right place for a ballgame; relatively speaking, you are in the middle of nowhere. To get to the park, you don't exit the "T" at Fenway, but at Kenmore Square which, strangely, has become a part of the ballpark. The strength and aura of the ballpark, the excitement generated within its drab exterior walls, is so powerful that it absorbs all that surrounds it, so that, in effect, that whole area of Boston's Kenmore Square and environs is really Fenway Park. The blocks around Fenway serve as a shoddy portal to the masterwork.

The brightly lit Citgo auto fuel sign that looms above Kenmore Square functions as a landmark so fans can find the place. Despite being at some remove from the ballpark proper, it exists as a totem and an integral part of Fenway's motif. In any other locale, it might be viewed as just another commercial blight on

England character. There has been no cosmetic work done and no major surgery to the structure save for the construction of luxury seating–which, ironically, provided economic support for the business of Red Sox baseball. In its turn, this has allowed the park to withstand the threat of demolition–a painless compromise to massive restorations changing the very nature of the original.

Like all treasures, Fenway Park is hard to find. Not exactly buried, but certainly hidden. From the outside, the edifice could be mistaken for an old time office building, at best. There is little on the exterior that hints of what is waiting through the turnstiles. Indeed, expectations are low, based on what is seen outside. But then who would expect the pearl glistening within the crusty oyster shell? There is no space around Fenway as with Dodger Stadium, and no parts of it loom up in the distance as with Yankee Stadium or SkyDome. Compared to Fenway, even

the landscape of a major city. In Boston it becomes part of the grand tableau of going to a Red Sox game. Likewise, the names of the streets surrounding Fenway have significance only in that they are associated with the ballpark. To walk around the park you have to make five turns to get back to where you started.

While Fenway stands, secure in its birthright, even the middle period parks of the 1950s and 60s are gone. Memorial in Baltimore, and County Stadium in Milwaukee, not bad, but gone, or soon to be, as are most of the others. Not timeless like Fenway. Candlestick? Riverfront in Cincinnati? Good riddance. Same for Pittsburgh's Three Rivers and the others that were built to satisfy the needs of professional football.

Fenway Park has been the flagship of the fleet, the crowning glory of a nation's great new contribution to its own newly developed sport. When Fenway was built, the American League had existed for only 12 years; the earliest big league, the National League as we know it, just 36 years. In 1912, Fenway would have best been considered "ballpark modern," just as the neoclassical Camden

Yards, Jacobs Field, and Coors are thought of today. We wonder: what it is about Fenway that has allowed it to survive when all those other palaces of the early days went to rubble long ago? Ebbets Field and the Polo Grounds were deserted by their teams, but why didn't Shibe Park survive, or Comiskey? Crosley and Forbes Fields have even been replaced by parks which are already obsolete, while Fenway still stands, functional, enduring and beloved.

In the 1970s, the Yankee braintrust saw fit to remove the delicate lattice from the lip of the Stadium roof—although that lattice was built as a part of the house for Babe Ruth. Such crass and thoughtless sacrilege would never happen at Fenway (they sold the Babe but they didn't trifle with the park.) There the love affair between Jean and Tom Yawkey is spelled out and preserved in Morse code on the scoreboard, surviving the decades since the time when wartime servicemen on leave would first decipher for other baseball romantics the esoteric love call. Boston respects and embraces its history.

When they added the rooftop areas at Fenway, the Red Sox trustees had no fancy notions of tarting up the place. They built up simple railroad shanties, solid and straight. Thus the spirit and personality were retained. How much more Puritan or Shaker in simplicity could it be to better mirror the New England character and satisfy the New England penchant for straightforwardness. How absolutely perfect. The ballpark is strong and durable, understated and purposeful.

And still Fenway stands. An anachronism in a city proud of its anachronisms, housing a sport proud of its anachronisms.

Fenway Saved

Perhaps what lies at the heart of the Fenway experience and the privilege of being there is this: winning is wonderful, but it isn't everything, and deep down we must accept the ludicrous notion that maybe, just maybe, the park is more important than the team, and more everlasting. Teams come and go while the great house continues to provide. Fans are willing to say that, "Yes, as New Englanders we will suffer for the sake of what is beautiful. It is our moral duty." The design is strong, with profound meaning. Its essence is to test those fans' resolve and their strength to abide.

Fenway, this wonder, this masterwork, this "green place," this glorious doyenne of ballyards, has entered the consciousness of North America. Those who have actually seen it and those who have only heard of it know that it is more than a field of play—it is Americana, and no less an integral and vital part of the cultural and aesthetic fabric of the United States than the nation's Capitol. It is a place from which we will never come back.

Fenway Saved

The Wall–1934

A Brief History of Fenway Park

Built in 1912, Fenway is the oldest park still in use for major league baseball. The very age which makes it so revered also renders it susceptible: it is at once enduring and endangered, venerable and highly vulnerable. It is revered for many reasons—nostalgia for simpler times, as a symbol of baseball tradition, for the unpretentious design of a ballpark built for the fans. It is endangered because it was built for another era, and the economics of professional sports franchises today make it extremely difficult to remain competitive playing in an older stadium.

There have been many renovations of Fenway over the years, including some significant ones. Through it all, though, the basic "footprint" of the playing field has remained more or less the same. This is the same field on which Babe Ruth played, and Ty Cobb, and "Shoeless" Joe Jackson, and Tris Speaker, not to mention Ted Williams, Joe DiMaggio, Carl Yastrzemski and countless others.

Though Fenway Park now seems to sit smack in the middle of downtown Boston, the city itself has evolved over time to make it so. Boston was originally a near-island connected only to the mainland by a thin strip of land called the Neck. To create more land, the three hills of Boston were graded down to provide landfill, which was then used to fill in an area now known as Back Bay.

The early Red Sox played at the Huntington Avenue Grounds, a park which was on a site currently occupied by part of Northeastern University. A statue of Cy Young on campus graces the spot where the mound once was. Young retired after the 1911 season, and so never played at Fenway.

The Charles River was a tidal river until dammed, and the area where Kenmore Square and Fenway Park are today, made up of marshland and mud flats, was therefore undeveloped. A vestige of the old Muddy River still flows, albeit sluggishly, under Commonwealth Avenue and highway overpasses leading onto Storrow Drive. Red Sox owner John I. Taylor looked at this area, and where others saw land unfit for use, he saw an opportunity for development. The Taylors also owned the *Boston Globe* until its sale to the New York Times Company in the early 1990s. Taylor wanted a new park for his team, primarily to enhance the marketability of the Red Sox franchise, and, indeed, he sold both the team, the land and the park just a few months

after construction began.

The Osborn Engineering Company of Cleveland was chosen to design Fenway Park, the same firm that went on to create Yankee Stadium, Braves Field, the Polo Grounds and other ballparks. Now the smallest facility in the majors, Fenway was sizable compared to other parks created in that era, and certainly not seen as the "lyric little bandbox" or "jewel box" it's sometimes characterized as today. In fact, some fans who followed the team from the Huntington Avenue Grounds—less than a mile away—griped that the new park was too big.

Fenway opened on April 20, 1912, within just a few days of the sinking of the *Titanic,* its parameters determined to some degree by the patterns of surrounding urban realities (streets, a railway, etc.). It was one of the very first ballparks built primarily from concrete and steel, though there were two "wings" of grandstand seats along each foul line made from traditional wood. "The park was quickly acclaimed as a great place to watch baseball," writes Michael Gershman in *Diamonds.* "The seats were oak, and the red brick facade, done in the Tapestry style, seemed to be almost needlepointed and reminded onlookers of a New England sampler."

The park had some unusual features, most notably "Duffy's Cliff" in left. In front of where the Green Monster is today, there was a ten foot high incline, on which fans could sit to watch the game. Fielders going after a deep fly would

could run up there, and even with a high fly ball, he could catch it. When that mound come down, he could never jump that high to catch that ball. It would go off The Wall.

"I'll never forget the day that someone hit a high fly ball to left field and Bob Fothergill, who played left field for us [the Tigers], he run about halfway up, fell down and the ball hit him right in the butt!

"Naturally, every ball hit out that way, I used to run out there because if it got by the outfielder, I used to keep the guy from taking the extra base. But this time I laughed, I was laughing so much, he said, 'What's so funny about it?' I says, 'Well, look at your face and then look at your butt. You've got a blue mark there.'"

A successor of Lewis's was the wonderfully named Smead Jolley, who terminated one of his early fielding efforts by sliding down the slope on his rear end. To the resultant dugout teasing he is supposed to have replied, "You smart guys taught me how to go up the hill, but nobody taught me how to come down."

Outfield defense was the forte of Tris Speaker, who recorded 35 assists in 1912. He played an incredibly shallow center, five times making unassisted double plays by grabbing liners or low flies and then stepping on second. He'd field a ball on one hop and throw runners out at first. Babe Ruth, a Red Sox pitcher for six seasons, called Speaker a "fifth infielder."

have to run up the slope and try to grab the ball. This oddity was named after Sox left fielder Duffy Lewis, who played there the first six years of Fenway's existence and proved very adept at negotiating the "cliff." One can imagine that such familiarity gave the Sox a certain home field advantage. Duffy's Cliff presented problems for Red Sox players, too, however.

Billy Rogell was a shortstop who played in the original park for the Red Sox in 1925, 1927 & 1928 and then as a visiting player for the Tigers from 1930 through 1939. Rogell, the oldest living Red Sox veteran, recalled at age 94 that visiting left fielders often had a difficult time with Duffy's Cliff. It was one of the early, unique features of Fenway that could provide a real edge for those who knew how to play it. It was one of Rogell's responsibilities as shortstop to be prepared to back up the left fielder, should the fielder fall or the ball take a wild bounce.

"When they had the mound up there [Duffy's Cliff], they used to be able to catch a lot of those balls that were, say, ten feet off the ground. Today, they don't catch those balls. At that time, a fellow

Advertising signs adorned the left field Wall as well as other available surfaces in the park, until 1947. Paying fans sometimes were permitted out onto the playing field itself in the deep outfields when all seats were taken, standing behind ropes drawn across to fence them off from action. It helped that the ball was much deader then, but in fact balls did reach the crowd from time to time. Most of the time fans weren't on the field, of course, but there were still oddities. A ball hit to center could bounce behind the right field bleachers, out of sight of the umpires, and yet remain in play while the center fielder scrambled after it.

When first unveiled, the 25-foot high wooden Wall which rose above Duffy's Cliff in left field seemed to be sufficiently far from the plate and sufficiently high that few expected balls to be hit out in that direction. It didn't take long, though, before someone did just that. Just six days after the park opened, the immortal Hugh "Corns" Bradley hit one clear out, over The Wall, over everything. Even he

must have been astonished. It was one of only two home runs he ever hit.

Still, home runs in any direction were rare occurrences in the days when ten would win you the home run title. Speaker tied for the league lead with Frank "Home Run" Baker in 1912; each hit 10 home runs. Baker's personal best, also a league leader, was in 1913, with 12. After thirteen years in AL ball, he had hit 96. The home run statistic itself was not one fans really doted upon the way they have ever since Babe Ruth began to post, well, Ruthian totals. Even as late as 1918, the most Ruth managed was 11. Not until the next year, his last in Boston, did his total jump to 29. In those days, triples were far more plentiful, and more prestigious, than homers; the leaders in three-baggers usually hit 2-3 times as many triples as the home run kings did round-trippers.

And Ruth started at Fenway, a fact all too well remembered even by Sox fans not born until decades later. Boston owner Harry Frazee—who had

actually helped finance some good Red Sox teams, culminating in the 1918 World Champions—ran into financial difficulties and was forced to sell Babe Ruth to the Yankees. The chief cause of the problem was the money he was spending on preparations for a Broadway play, later infamous in the minds of Sox purists, called *No No Nanette*. The show, once properly launched, became a big hit and made Frazee a reputed two million dollars. But the Babe was gone, and when Frazee sold the team itself, the new owners of the Red Sox had very little money left for player development or park maintenance.

The Ruth trade laid the foundation for a Yankee dynasty and supplanted what had really been a decade and a half of Boston dominance. The Yankees never looked back. Red Sox fans believe there exists a "Curse of the Bambino," a curse which has plagued their team ever since this baseball blasphemy. This is seen by otherwise rational human beings as the only possible explanation for a championship drought of over eighty years. It is a dry spell marked by an incredible number of especially cruel last minute failings which have cost championships time and time again. Periodic efforts by rock radio stations and others to exorcise the Curse have thus far proven fruitless.

Incredibly, the Yankees got more than Babe Ruth. They even owned the mortgage on Fenway Park itself. Frazee mortgaged the Park and grounds to Boston's rivals for an additional $350,000 over and above the money paid for Ruth. A few years later,

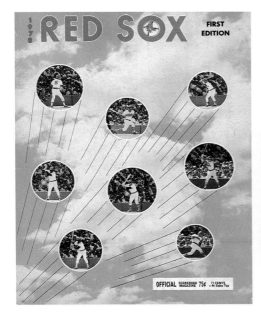

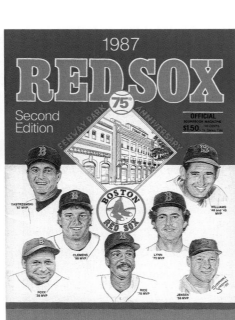

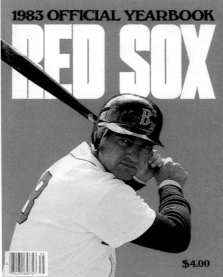

baseline being much more incestuous back then, Frazee sold the team to Bob Quinn, the GM of the St. Louis Browns. The team continued to languish with perpetually under-capitalized ownership until young (and very wealthy) Thomas A. Yawkey bought the Boston Red Sox in 1933.

Languish is perhaps not a strong enough word for it—the team finished in last place 8 out of 9 times between 1922 and 1930, only rising above it once (in 1924, when they edged out the White Sox by a half game to finish in 7th place.) In 1931, they moved up to 6th place but, alas, they were back in the cellar after the 1932 season 64 games out of first, with a record of 43 wins and 111 losses. The Red Sox had drawn a total attendance of 182,150 in 1932 and it's not surprising that Quinn was willing to relinquish ownership. One of Yawkey's first moves was to renovate Fenway Park. Major changes were effected, the greatest makeover in the park's history.

Osborn Engineering was again brought in. Duffy's Cliff was removed and the wooden wall replaced by a 37 foot high barricade composed of wooden railroad ties covered with tin and set atop a concrete base. Until 1976, this structure was lacking any kind of protective padding. There remained for some years a slight grade in front of The Wall which served as an early warning track (the clay track was not installed until much later.) The old wooden bleachers which had burned down in 1926 and had never been replaced were now reconstructed, this time out of concrete and steel. The grandstands along the foul lines were made of similar materials.

Even today, Fenway stands remain close to the action. There is very little foul territory, another reason pitchers find it so tough. Some front row seats are as close to the plate as the pitcher's mound, even a few inches less—just sixty feet. By contrast, Yankee Stadium's home plate is some 84 feet from the closest seats.

A manual scoreboard was also created, set into the left field wall, during the 1934 renovation, and one could follow the scores of the eight teams in each league. (In 1976, The Wall was redone, covered with hard fiberglass-like plastic which resulted in truer caroms. Padding was added along its base, and the National League portion of the scoreboard was removed, the entire board itself being then recentered on The Wall by shifting it to the right.)

Due to the number of balls hit over The Wall and through windows in buildings on the other side of Lansdowne Street, two years after the 1934 renovation a net just over 23 feet high was added to the top of The Wall.

Yawkey created a modern baseball park, one which has grown old gracefully. A ballpark so successful, and so beloved, that the current Yawkey Trust management is finding it hard to convince the public it is time to replace it.

Tom Yawkey was owner of the Red Sox for over 40 years, from 1934 until 1976, when he died. His wife Jean then continued to own the team—and was a fixture one could see in the owner's box virtually every game—until her own death in 1992. The Yawkeys loved Fenway Park and even spent time there when the Red Sox were not in town. Together, they owned and ran the Boston Red Sox for nearly sixty years, and the JRY Trust created by Jean R. Yawkey still owns the team today, though under a mandate to sell within a certain period of time, the revenues to go to specified charities.

Tom Yawkey created a team which contended, and a ballpark which engendered an enduring love and affection from generations of Red Sox fans. A ballpark for the ages.

During Tom Yawkey's tenure as owner, the Sox fielded some classic teams and came tantalizingly close to winning the pennant and World Series several times. His stewardship of Fenway Park, which Jean Yawkey continued after his death, was exemplary. The adaptations made by the Yawkeys fell into two categories, those of a progressive nature—such as adding lighting for night games—and those of a conservative, neo-traditional nature—such as removing advertising from the park to focus attention exclusively on the field of play.

In 1939, when rookie Ted Williams hit 14 home

With the billboards gone, it was easier to follow the flight of the ball. The coats of paint also seemed to add new energy, as baseballs skittered merrily off eight different wall angles in fair territory, two doorways and the ladder. The result was crowd-pleasing unpredictability, what poet Donald Hall called 'a huge pinball machine designed by a mad sculptor.'"
— Gershman, DIAMONDS

runs into the distant right field seats, Yawkey, perhaps sensing he had his own fledgling Babe Ruth, decided to shorten the distance from home plate by having bullpens installed in right. This was accomplished in 1940 and came to be known as "Williamsburg." Rooftop seats were also added in the 1940s.

In 1947, lighting towers were erected and the era of night baseball began. The Monster became the Green Monster, as advertisements on the left field Wall for Calvert whiskey, Gem razor blades and Lifebuoy soap were removed. As Sox teams

Clear Heads Choose **Calvert**
THE WHISKEY WITH THE HAPPY BLENDING

Avoid 5 o'clock Shadow

GEM
SINGLEDGE BLADES

GULF

July 4, 1942 Yankees vs. Red Sox

improved, it was probably good to get rid of the old Lifebuoy sign; fans picked up on the slogan "The Red Sox use it" and commented on how they sure needed it! The signs also removed a distraction to fielders. Doc Cramer once lost a ball off The Wall in the colors of the advertising. The entire left field Wall was painted its distinctive dark green.

The only slightly frivolous touch running contrary to the conservative trend was that owner Yawkey added his initials and those of his wife, to the scoreboard in left. However, since they were discreetly (almost invisibly) printed vertically, and in Morse code, it wasn't exactly a gaudy display of their affections. Like initials carved into some great oak, they remain there at the close of the millenium as a symbol of their mutual admiration.

As time passed, additional wall advertising was removed from the park, so that eventually only one sign remained—the almost sacred Jimmy Fund billboard in right field. The sign for the Red Sox' special charity was the sole bit of advertising in the park for about 25 years.

The broadcast booth was erected over the screen in the early 1950s, and the organ which John Kiley played for so many years was added in 1959. In 1970, the old flagpole which stood, in play, in center field was removed and re-positioned to the location where it currently stands.

Tom Yawkey was a baseball purist and most of the significant changes, other than the conservative ones, came at the time of, or after, his death. Aside from a few adjustments to the fences and the

like, the end of the Tom Yawkey era saw the park remain very much as it had been reconstructed, with relatively few significant changes. Despite the untold millions of dollars he invested in the Red Sox, perhaps that is Tom Yawkey's greatest, and most enduring, contribution to Boston baseball.

In the 1980s there were further renovations of Fenway, much more substantial than the 1975-76 replacement of The Wall and installation of the electronic video scoreboard over the bleachers. In 1983, an array of luxury roof boxes were installed, and in 1988 the current "600 Club" and new press box/media facilities were added. Wade Boggs and others argued that the wind patterns within Fenway were changed dramatically as a result. Starting early in the 1990s, the bathroom facilities were upgraded. By 1991, bowing to changing times and the make up of the crowds, a diaper changing station was added in the first aid room under the right field grandstand. Co-author Bill Nowlin's son Emmet was, as it happened, the first infant to make use of this part of Fenway Park. Curiously, no plaque yet marks that historic moment.

Before the 1997 season, large Coca-Cola bottles were placed on one of the light standards over The Wall. Some were scandalized, though of course the Sox were simply reverting to a bit of the older tradition when advertisements covered The Wall. On Opening Day 1997, the first home run tattooed a Coke bottle.

Before the 1998 season began, a modest rearrangement of the retired number sequence on the

right field grandstand roof was effected. Previously, the numbers had read, in sequence, 9-4-1-8 to reflect the order in which the numbers of four players had been retired: Ted Williams, Joe Cronin, Bobby Doerr and Carl Yastrzemski. Number 42 was added, in 1997, to reflect the game-wide retirement of Jackie Robinson's #42. Between the 1997 and 1998 seasons, though, the Red Sox undertook to take down the numbers and re-sequence them numerically. Perhaps they had tired of hearing the bit of urban folklore that the numbers 9-4-1-8 meant 9/4/18, and stood for the last time the Red Sox had won the World Series.

> *Ted Williams credited the relative "cleanness" of the park for much of his success:*
>
> *"The biggest thing going for me to hit .400 was Fenway Park in Boston, and before you question the logic of that, let me explain. First it has a good, green background. Mr. Yawkey kept all the signs out, everything was green. There were no shadows. And then there was that short, high fence in left field. You say, but Williams was a pull hitter to right field. That's correct. But it gave me a different kind of advantage. Even though I didn't hit out that way, I always said to myself, If you swing a little late it won't be the worst thing in the world, because there's that short fence, the defense isn't there, and slices or balls hit late can still go out.*
>
> *"So I didn't worry about hitting late, and what did that do for me? It allowed me to develop the most valuable luxury a hitter can have: the ability to wait on the ball. By waiting, you get fooled less by the pitch. By waiting, and being quick with the bat, you can protect the plate with two strikes. You can follow the ball better."* [My Turn at Bat]

"Truly, The Wall is baseball's Lorelei, luring all hitters with its beauty and apparent accessibility and ruining many when they fall for it."–Al Hirshberg

THE WALL

Think Fenway, and you think, The Wall.

It's the park's defining characteristic. Located a mere 310 (or so) feet from home plate, the 37-foot high Green Monster has become one of North America's better known landmarks. Some writers have even dared mention it in the same breath as the Great Wall of China; others, perhaps more appropriately in the case of the Red Sox, with Jerusalem's Wailing Wall. It was erected decades before the Berlin Wall and still stands, ten years after that even more notorious slab of concrete became a footnote to history.

There are two oft-repeated truisms in Boston baseball lore about The Wall. "The Wall giveth and The Wall taketh away" is one of them; the other is, "those who live by The Wall die by The Wall."

HITTERS

"The team's strategy has been a prisoner of Fenway, or at least of The Wall. Big-boom right handed hitters were always coveted (many of whom dented The Wall for singles), even though the most productive hitters at Fenway have been left handed–Williams, Yastrzemski, Wade Boggs. The hit-and-run remains a rarity and the stolen base a sacrilege."
— *Martin Nolan,* The Red Sox Reader

The Sox have often tried to build teams around the promise of a particular right-handed slugger. These designer teams seldom worked out. Invariably it is the left handed Red Sox hitter–Ruth, Williams, Yaz, Boggs, Vaughn–who has more success at Fenway.

A right-handed power hitter like a Jim Rice or a Jimmie Foxx could strike terror into the hearts of an opposing pitcher. They didn't need a Green Monster to aid them. In *The Picture History of the Boston Red Sox, George* Sullivan recounts that Lefty Gomez wore glasses one day at Fenway but discarded them after just one inning. "Sure, I could see out of them," Gomez said. "That was the trouble–I could see too damn well. I nearly had a heart attack when that Foxx came to the plate. I never knew he was *that* big. Then I looked out at that left field Wall and almost had another cardiac. I never knew it was *that* close. So to hell with the

pop fly out in virtually every other park in baseball—just made the net on top of The Wall as it descended. "Talk about loving Fenway Park so much. I hated Fenway Park when Dent hit that home run," admits former Red Sox pitching ace Jim Lonborg. It may just be a trick of memory, or a symptom of the Red Sox fan's natural cynicism—there was, after all, Fisk's dramatic Game Six home run in the 1975 World Series—but it often seems that the Red Sox have been hurt more by The Wall than they have been helped by it. It is a subject that will forever be debated over hot stoves from Old Greenwich to Aroostook County, and beyond.

One thing is certain, familiarity with The Wall helps Red Sox players both offensively and defensively: offensively because veteran Sox hitters know from the way the ball hits

glasses. What I don't know won't hurt me."

Despite the many sluggers the Sox have paraded into town over the years, it often took a Bucky Dent to prove the point that those who live by The Wall must die by it. Dent's 1978 playoff game home run—a fairly routine

whether to try for that extra base; defensively because left fielders know each carom that The Wall produces. Nonetheless, the number of disastrous moves which Sox ownership has made to bring in power hitters, thinking they would take full advantage of all The Wall has

to offer, probably has more than outweighed the benefits of that familiarity. Only in the last decade has ownership seemed to have fought off this temptation.

The Sox did bring right handed sluggers to Bos-ton, and in some cases it paid off. Bobby Doerr was a good example. When he came up in 1937, the Red Sox made him a pull hitter to take advan-tage of the Green Monster, It worked, and Bobby hit 223 home runs in his fourteen years in the ma-jors, all with the Red Sox.

It may have worked better for a doubles hitter such as Doerr than with a natural slugger, like George Scott. "Boomer" got too enamored with The Wall and that proved to be his downfall. As a rookie in 1966, he hit 27 home runs, followed by 19 in his sophomore season. But then, according to one observer, he got "chummy with The Wall", and it turned its back on him as he hit only three home runs in 1968. In fact, he had his career high of 36 home runs when he was playing in Milwaukee, not Boston.

Tom Yawkey himself was not above lamenting the effect The Wall had on his team. "We've done very well at home," he said in 1965. "If we'd been able to play .500 ball on the road we'd have been a lot higher [in the standings.] But damn it, that Wall hurts; it has an effect on the organization from top to bottom. We have to go after players who have that Fenway stroke, but then they get in the habit of pulling the ball and they try it on the road—in Yankee Stadium or in Comiskey—and it's no good. Hitters' habits are hard to break."

It's not hard to find right handed Red Sox hitters who have experienced heartbreak at Fenway. Tony Conigliaro was one who dominated in his home park, reaching the 100 home run plateau at a younger age than any player in history up to that time. The local hero also lost his share of homers, however. Former Yankee pitcher Ralph Terry recalls one of Conigliaro's drives: "Tony C. hit a rocket off me that was probably the hardest ball ever hit off me, much harder than anything I remember. It was rising, almost like it was picking up speed, when it smashed into The Wall

The Wall

about two feet from the top. There was this crash, like a car accident, and then the ball dropped straight down. We held him to a single. If that Wall wasn't there, I swear that ball would have gone over five hundred feet."

Many a home run ball has become simply a long single at Fenway. Balls hit sharply off The Wall which would have gone out in any other park, can—if played well—be fired into second holding the batter to one base. Larry Gardner, the first third baseman to play for the Sox in Fenway, was actually thrown out before he got to first, on a ball hit off The Wall.

Successful Sox teams have usually not been built on the long ball. In fact, the 1967 Impossible Dream team was notable for its lack of right handed power. Focusing on The Wall could arguably have killed the 1967 team, had they tried to feed off it. As Al Hirshberg has famously written, "Truly, The Wall is baseball's Lorelei, luring all hitters with its beauty and apparent accessibility and ruining many when they fall for it."

For all that The Wall has hurt, though, Fenway Park is still considered a hitter's park. According to Thorn & Palmer's *The Hidden Game of Baseball*, the "park factor" at Fenway produces 13 percent more offense than other parks.

"I don't know how many home runs I've lost on account of playing in this ballpark. Dozens, I guess. Dozens and dozens. I hit line drives off The Wall a lot of times that would be home runs in other parks. They're rising, see, as they hit The Wall. Then I lose home runs on fly balls to center field, all those three-hundred-ninety-foot fly balls. Fenway [would have been] perfect for me if you reversed the dimensions. Put The Wall in right.'"
— *Dwight Evans, former Red Sox right fielder*

Fenway Saved

"Rookies drool when they see The Wall...it kindles a twinkle in the eye of banjo hitters, instant mental spinach to make them feel like sluggers." — George Sullivan

PITCHERS

"Think about The Wall?
You don't think about
anything else."
— Bill Monbouquette

If it's true that Fenway does foster greater offensive output, it's only natural that pitchers should fear and loathe the Green Monster. Bob Feller, a Hall of Fame hurler with the Cleveland Indians, became a mere mortal at Fenway. "I seldom pitched well at Fenway Park. I think I had a complex about it going back to that first game there when I was 17. I looked at that left field Wall and felt hemmed in. I knew Cronin and Foxx could pop it over with half a swing." Even Ted Williams, whose disdain for pitchers is legendary, is uncharacteristically sympathetic toward those who take the mound at Fenway. "You can have a pitcher pitching just a whale

"It was the very day that Lou Boudreau first used the "Boudreau Shift" or the "Williams Shift"–July 14, 1946. Ted had hit three home runs in the first game of the doubleheader at Fenway. "Between innings during the first game, with 35,000 people in the park, all–that day–screaming accolades at Williams, Ted, instead of going to the bench stepped into the score board in left field, and slipped out a trapdoor into the street. In full baseball regalia, he calmly trotted to a nearby cafeteria and ordered a plate of ice cream. Then, before the waiter had recovered from this surprise, Williams rushed back to the park, went in the same door he had used going out and stepped out to his position in left field in time for the next inning."
— Al Hirshberg, The Red Sox, The Bean, and The Cod

of a ballgame, and someone gets up there and bloops one off The Wall, and the whole game changes," he says.

Generations of pitchers have lost sleep attempting to solve the dilemma of pitching in the unfriendly confines of Fenway. Southpaws were especially susceptible to insomnia because few left handers were ever successful in Boston. Even a Hall of Famer like the Yankees' Whitey Ford sported a lofty 6.16 ERA in Fenway. One lefty who was successful there was Bill Lee. As he wrote in his book *The Wrong Stuff,* "A left hander's first good look at the left field Wall, the Green Monster in Fenway, is an automatic reason for massive depression. And that's when viewed from the dugout. From the vantage point of the mound it looms even closer. I felt like I was scraping my knuckles against it every time I went into motion, and I was always afraid that it would fall down and kill Rico Petrocelli at short. That Wall psyched out a lot of good pitchers. Great control pitchers would come into Fenway and suddenly not have it that day... It's just not a park built with the welfare of pitchers in mind. The key to pitching at Fenway, whether you are right handed or left handed but especially if you're a lefty, is to keep the ball outside and away on right handers and down and in to left handers... You can make the temptation of The Wall work for you. The Monster giveth, but the Monster taketh away. You just have to know what to feed it."

Fenway Saved

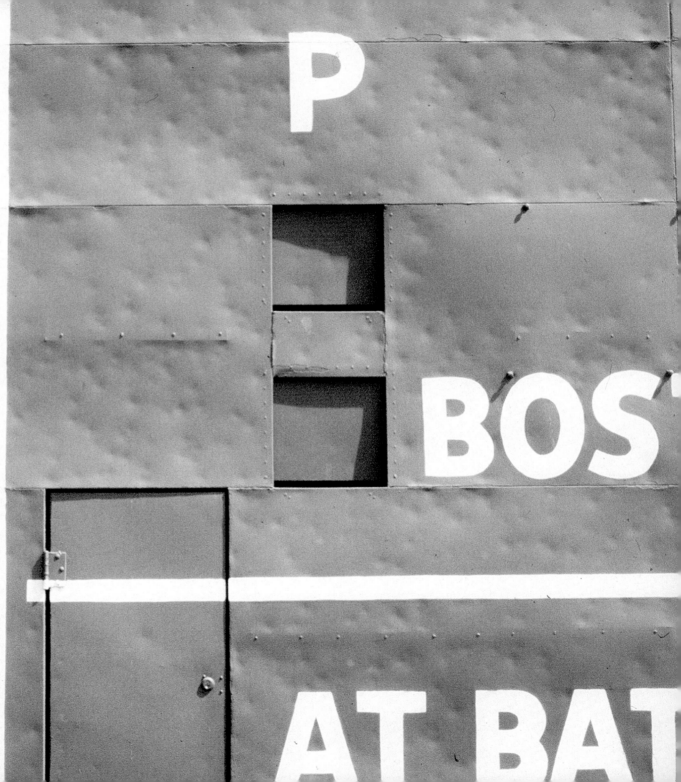

Both pitchers and hitters tend to alter their natural style of play to take account of The Wall, and this often affects their play when they are away from Fenway. George Higgins suggests that much of the southpaw fear of Fenway is unfounded. "True, the pitchers must take into account the various dimensions of the parks and adjust their deliveries accordingly when calling upon hosts with shallow power alleys. But few pitchers endeavor to throw fly balls anyway, especially to right handed batters in Fenway—what they want are grounders."

Jim Lonborg, a 22-game winner for the '67 American League Champion Red Sox offers a right hander's perspective: "You know, sometimes I think the mentality of a pitcher is that you don't focus in on the dimensions of the park that you're pitching in. You really try to focus in on the importance of making your specific pitches, from inning to inning. After the game, you can look back and think, 'If I would have been at Dodger Stadium instead of Fenway Park, I would have won the game' or something, because of the presence of The

Wall.

"I think probably, as a group, left handers might have felt more a presence of The Wall than right handers, because they were constantly aware of right handed hitters looking to pull the ball. And if they didn't have the kind of skills that allowed them to pitch right handed hitters inside, they were definitely going to get penalized. Not every pitcher, whether he's a right hander or left hander, knows how to pitch to the inside part of the plate."

Mel Parnell, one of the greatest Sox southpaws ever (his 1956 no-hitter at Fenway was the first spun there in thirty years), confirms Lonborg's assessment:

"Pitching at Fenway was different from other parks because of the short left field fence. You had to be very careful. You couldn't come down the middle of the plate, because if you did, you were in danger. The hitter could then swing with his arms extended and he'd get full strength in his swing. It didn't take a real momentous clout to get over that left field Wall—a long fly ball could just carry over. For that reason, I kept the ball in tight on the hitter trying to keep him swinging with his elbows as close to his body as possible. That way he wasn't swinging with extended arms and he was sacrificing strength, swinging at pitches on the inside part of the plate. Many times pitches that were off the inside corner of the plate, they'd still swing at them because they could see the pitch there [at Fenway] pretty good and they were trying to hit it out of the ballpark.

"The lack of foul territory at Fenway Park was even more important than The Wall. There's nothing much down the left field line, as a matter of fact there's nothing at all hardly, other than about three feet. Down in right field, your line doesn't run all the way down to the very end. It cuts off fairly short and that leaves very little foul territory there. And there isn't much depth between home plate and the back screen. Any foul ball has a good chance of going into the seats, so you lose a lot of outs. You would get outs in other ballparks, where the hitter is getting another swing of the bat at you in Fenway."

Charlie Wagner adds his two cents' worth: "You had to know how to pitch in Fenway. A lot of guys were afraid to throw change-ups, and it's one of the best pitches in the world to throw because everybody's looking for fastballs. The Wall doesn't bother you as much as the fact that you don't get the foul outs. Sometimes you'd get a guy two strikes and you'd throw him the pitch that you thought you could get him out on, and he'd foul it, maybe pop it up back in the stands. You'd throw a good pitch and it just hits the top of the damn dugout or something like that. You couldn't foul out. So the pitcher would have to throw that extra pitch all the time. That's what got you in trouble. It's not The Wall.

"And the home runs that hit over The Wall or into the net are going to be home runs anyway. It's the ball that scrapes The Wall, that's the one that bothers you. The ball that hits The Wall like that would get caught in a lot of other ballparks. When I see Oakland, jeez, you could pitch there all day."

In the end, the other "Monster" probably had it right. Dick (The Monster) Radatz: "I think The Wall is the great equalizer. Sure, you lose some home runs over it, but there's a lot of guys, Al Kaline and Mantle come to mind, who'd rap shots off The Wall that would wind up as singles that might have been doubles or triples somewhere else. It balances out."

Lastly, Fielders

"If someone was trying to drive a left fielder nuts, this [The Wall] was just the way to do it."
— *Carl Yastrzemski, former Red Sox left fielder*

Some cynics might say that before a manager sends any left fielder out to stand in front of The Wall, he should first be issued a blindfold and a last cigarette, because it often represents a very public execution. Indeed, as balls leave the barrel of the bat to ricochet off the Green Monster, left fielders might almost prefer taking their chances with a real firing squad (others might suggest that along with adding padding to The Wall, they might well have provided straitjackets for visiting outfielders.) Left and center fielders since the days of Duffy Lewis have had to develop special talents to cope with Fenway's eccentric left field Wall. Judging how deep the ball might carry can require constant awareness of changing weather conditions, and judging the carom on a ball hit off The Wall requires a sense of geometry, physics, and perhaps a semester of Psych 101.

The Green Monster has the only "in-play" ladder in baseball and occasionally a ball will strike the ladder itself, and take a crazy bounce. Jim Lemon

got an inside-the-park home run off one such ricochet. Dick Stuart, no speed demon on the base paths, had one himself off a dramatically high fly ball which, when it finally came down, took a wild bounce off the top of the scoreboard.

For over 40 years, two fielders, and only two, regularly patrolled left for the Red Sox: they were Ted Williams and Carl Yastrzemski. It would be comforting to think that they both got their reward for such hardship duty with election to the Hall of Fame, but their hitting abilities may also have contributed. Ted and Yaz have expressed quite different views of The Wall. It should come as no surprise that while many fans certainly enjoy the quirks and eccentricities of Fenway with all its angles, the same does not necessarily hold true for the players who actually work the field. In general, Williams favors a more predictable field while Yaz claimed to love The Wall for that same unpredictability.

Many have written that Williams was a sub-par fielder, but this was not the consensus of his contemporaries, whose judgment should be paramount. In fact, Ted studied wall defense, as did committed fielders who have followed in his footprints. George Higgins suggests that the lack of appreciation for Williams' defensive prowess was partly because he played The Wall with such apparent ease, bordering on nonchalance. "It was fashionable to sneer at Williams as a fielder when I was a kid because he was unpopular in the press and because he had studied The Wall the way Einstein studied relativity. He seldom had to hurry much to field any

carom—so he was charged with jaking it, lollygagging around and dreaming while awaiting his next turn at bat. That was a bad rap."

David Falkner, in his study of baseball's great glove men, *Nine Sides of the Diamond,* gives vivid accounts of the treachery to be found in Boston's left field and gives Williams high marks for his field-

ing. "He learned The Wall with the same diligence he learned the strike zone—and for roughly the same reason: pride, a fierce, finicky desire to be the best at what he did." Dom DiMaggio, who played next to Ted in center for many years, agreed. " He knew as much about the left field Wall at Fenway as he did about hitting."

Al Hirshberg believes that The Wall has helped the Red Sox more defensively than it has offensively. He cites both Williams and Yastrzemski as strong fielders who made The Wall their ally. In *What's the Matter with the Red Sox?*, he wrote, "Both studied The Wall until they knew every little nick, every possible carom, and where to station themselves to get a ball bouncing off it. Yastrzemski, more agile and with a better arm, knew The Wall so well he could play tricks on hitters. Whenever a ball was hit to left, he could tell almost exactly where it would hit or if it would clear the fence. If it were headed for the screen, he did nothing, because there was nothing he could do—it was gone for a home run. But if the ball was going to carom off the fence out of his reach, with a man on base, Yastrzemski was marvelous at faking a catch he knew he couldn't make, standing at the place where he was sure the ball would come down."

The structure and composition of The Wall changed over the years, and the bounces or caroms gradually became more consistent and therefore more predictable. Carl Yastrzemski played both in the "tin era" and the "fiberglass one." He takes obvious pride in his working relationship with The Wall.

Yaz did acknowledge that Ted taught him how, since every ball comes off The Wall at an angle, "you've got to play every ball three to five feet to the right of where it hits."

Mike Greenwell worked hard at learning to play the caroms. "At least once every home stand Greenwell goes to The Wall and has a coach hit 50–75 balls off The Wall–off every part of it–off the corner by the foul pole, off the scoreboard, the low concrete base, the midsection of padding, the upper layers of metal stripping."–Falkner

"I came to love Fenway," Yaz wrote in *Yaz: Baseball, The Wall, and Me.* "It was a place that rejuvenated me after a road trip: the fans right on top of you, the nutty angles. And The Wall. That was my baby, the left field Wall. The Green Monster. You

know, when I started playing it that Wall had rivets sticking out of it, it had two-by-fours, it had tin. It had a concrete base that rose about twenty-five feet or so. And you had to know that a ball hit by a left handed batter would spin off it differently from a right hander's shot. I'm not even taking into account what would happen when it hit an exposed rivet. Or the two-by-fours. Or the tin. Or the holes in the scoreboard. Nowadays, The Wall is covered with fiberglass. It's practically playable. Playing The Wall changed tremendously when they went to fiberglass. It got easier. I hated that, because so much of the Red Sox tradition involves The Wall. Instead, the fiberglass gave everything a truer bounce. With the tin, nobody could figure it out. You could hit a million fungoes and it wouldn't help. It was all instinct."

From his rookie season until his retirement, Yaz employed that instinct better than anyone before or since. With his gifts of perception, speed and agility, he played The Wall like Chopin played a polonaise, as Joe Fitzgerald wrote. Ralph Kiner recalls a deke Yaz pulled in his rookie year. "It was one of the great plays I've ever seen. Minoso hit one towards the fence and Yaz positioned himself to play the rebound—only there was no rebound. At the last second, Yaz turned around and caught the ball, completely fooling the runner and everyone in the place,

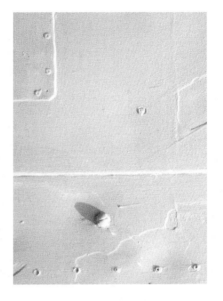

who thought for sure the ball was well up on The Wall. He threw into the infield for an easy double play. How was he able to do that? Because he knew the park so well and because he had to be thinking about it ahead of time." Yaz won seven Gold Gloves and led the majors in assists for seven years as well. No easy task for someone patrolling left at Fenway Park for half his career.

"I had a decoy move for every situation. If I knew, for example, that the runner on base was slow, and the ball was going to hit off The Wall, I'd set up as if I was going to catch the ball. That would freeze the runner off the bag with a short lead. Then suddenly I'd turn around, grab the rebound off The Wall, and throw to the next base, or home. The trick was, I had to catch the rebound clean off The Wall. All the deking in the world wouldn't help if the ball got past me, or if I bobbled it, or if it came to me on a bounce. The Wall got to be a game with me. I had to develop more tricks to be effective. Word got around the league about what I was doing. So I decided to deke a guy only if the game was on the line."
— *Carl Yastrzemski*, Yaz: Baseball, The Wall, and Me

The Green Monster has many inherent booby-traps, and these—combined with other features in left, particularly in the way the ball can ricochet around off the adjacent large doorway which opens onto the field from under sections 32 and 33, or off the low wall grandstand that seems to jut out into left—affect the whole of a left fielder's defense preparation.

The closeness of The Wall held implications for the infielders as well, as Ted Williams remembers. "Any ball down the line meant the shortstop had to come out [to make a relay throw]. If it hit the tin, it dropped straight down; if it hit the cement, it would bounce back hard. If it hit a bolt, anything could happen." Former shortstop Johnny Pesky considers the issue from the perspective of an infielder: "I remember when I first got here [Fenway], Cronin grabbed me and said, 'Johnny, on any ball hit down the line, you've got to get out there. It might hit that Wall.' Well, a lot of times, it did hit that Wall, and the hitter would think he has a double but the ball came back to you, and suddenly you're taking maybe 50 or 60 steps away from him. I've thrown a lot of guys out there. It's something that a shortstop will learn

various possibilities and concluded that given the distinct likelihood that the fielder might "look like a perfect fool in front of 30,000 unsympathetic judges you understand why left field in Boston is sometimes seen as baseball's Valhalla, the hall of the slain."

In the end, playing The Wall came down to thoughtful preparation and practice, and occasionally a bit of luck. There were sure to be wild bounces, but you couldn't let The Wall play you. The final word goes to Joe DiMaggio who casually

suggested, in the face of the previous overwhelming evidence to the contrary: "The Monster was all psychological, all in the head." Easy for him to say; the Yankee star didn't have to play it, didn't have to pitch with it at his back, and as a lifetime .325 pull hitter, didn't have to think much about it at all, except to worry whether his doubles would end up as singles.

quickly, a very small thing, but something that happens almost every day. You try not to give the guy an extra base. If the ball hits, especially in that corner at Fenway, you've got to get your fanny out there. If you have a fine arm like Garciaparra, you can make plays. You can save yourselves a number of runs during the season."

In fact, it was and is a tough field to play for anyone. There's the unusual and unpredictable playing surface. There's the varying wind currents and swirls (perhaps more treacherous since the 1988 addition of the 600 Club and new media facilities.)

There is the traverse of sunlight and shadow across the field during the course of a day game. The fielder has a bit less reaction time due to the proximity to the plate, and then there is the near total absence of foul territory, all of this combined with the spectre of a couple of thousand loud and boisterous fans practically on top of you. (John Updike has written that certain fans would buy left field tickets just to verbally abuse Williams.) Joe Fitzgerald recounted all the

The Wall is a Monster, a totality of surface, netting and scoreboard. The scoreboard, the oldest manually operated scoreboard in baseball, presented a treacherous playing surface but also provided some unexpected amenities, making it seem almost human, even capable of communication. To stay loose, Williams would often chat with the scoreboard operator. The casual observer might think he was talking to The Wall itself rather than through the one inch by ten inch slits cut into the scoreboard. Dom DiMaggio recalls following his brother's 56-game hitting streak in 1941 with scoreboard operator assistance: "I was able to keep up-to-the-minute on Joe's streak when we were playing at home. Ted was friendly with the man who operated the scoreboard in left field at Fenway Park, Bill Daley. Each time my brother would get a hit, Daley would holler out to Ted in left field through an opening in the score board, and then Ted would yell over to me, "Hey, Dom! Joe just got a double!"

THE GROUNDS

"We, it appears, are to learn of high things, if at all, through the little things, and things of low estate. If we are to see the vision of the Grail, however dimly, it must no longer be in some vaulted chamber in a high tower of Carbonnek, over dreadful rocks and the foam of a faery sea..." [Arthur Machen, The Art of Wandering. London: Village Press, 1924.]

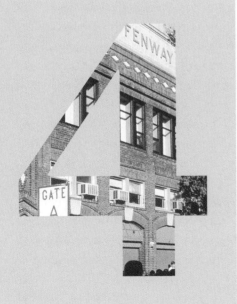

It is fall in New England and the leaves swirling across the pavement and the nip in the air foretell the imminent arrival of winter. Outside Fenway Park the streets are all but empty, save for a few curious baseball pilgrims from out of town. Gone are the sausage vendors, the program hawkers, the ticket scalpers furtively hustling their contraband. The entrances to the ballpark are barred with seeming permanence and the brick exterior looks cold and uninviting. Fenway lies dormant.

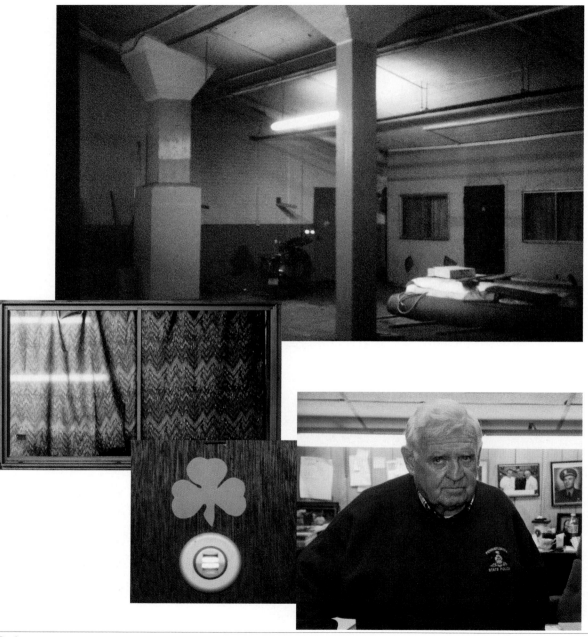

Well, not quite. Within these walls, beneath the grandstand, deep in the bowels of the park, sits a strange little cottage complete with curtained windows and a door with a shamrock on it. Inside, at a cluttered desk, sits Joe Mooney. The door is closed and the window curtains drawn but that doesn't matter because no sunlight could possibly penetrate this netherworld. In fact, Mr. Mooney (as he is often respectfully addressed) has arrived for work before daybreak and won't leave until well after the sun has set. There is little in this setting to suggest that Joe Mooney is the man responsible for keeping Fenway Park green and vibrant. Who would suspect that the splendor and beauty that is Fenway Park would emanate from such somber quarters, and from such an unpretentious man as this?

For over a quarter of a century, Joseph Mooney has been the unsung guardian of the Green Grail known as Fenway Park. From his humble workplace, he creates and maintains the impeccable beauty that fans have come to expect when journeying to Fenway. The green of the walls, the red and blue of the seats, the eau-de-Nil of the concourse, put it all down to Mooney. This gruff-exteriored, soft-centered Irishman lays down the law and he gives no quarter to carelessness. Like a battle-scarred field general, he commands his small battalion of helpers.

This crusty leprechaun would seem an unlikely possessor of such a gentle, nurturing touch—and such a keen, instinctive appreciation for Fenway's inherent glamour. He has never been tempted to

tamper with Fenway's style, only to insure that her timeless beauty is shown off to best advantage every day. He dresses her in her finery during the season but cloaks her in more practical garb to withstand the wintry blast. Thus is the winter of our discontent made glorious summer by this son of Scranton, Pennsylvania.

Winter comes even to Fenway Park. It is the season when the demons of precipitation would do harm. And so, just as the ballpark walls are wrapped in pliable green material to protect our diamond heroes from injury, so too the very field itself is covered to protect it from off-season inclemencies, from ice and snow and other natural enemies of baseball. The outfield is wrapped in white felt. Who can conceive of such kindness to Kentucky bluegrass? Who ordains it? Mooney, sitting at his desk in his sunless Fenway underworld decrees that it must be done, and that is enough. Before Christmas each year, Joe Mooney swathes the Fenway grass in pure white felt, like some bizarre Christmas present to Mother Nature. A practical man, he sees no symbolism in the act, no ritual of purification. It is carried out simply to protect the valuable real estate with which he is entrusted. "We cover it

Fenway Park is "a ballpark that is conducive to humor...Strange things happen out there. We've had a dog, a cat, a rabbit, birds of all kinds. I don't know where they come from."
— *Sherm Feller in* Forever Fenway

up with white felt, in December, for the winter," he says. "Maybe 3/16 of an inch, not even that. It keeps the ground from freezing. I get it made by the Harry Meller Company here. When it snows, we move the snow off. We clean the whole track all

the way around. So once it melts, it won't go to ice."

Mooney's official title is "Superintendent of Grounds and Maintenance" in which capacity he has served his Red Sox employers for the last 28 years, during which time the outfield sod has been replaced only infrequently. "We do it every twelve or thirteen years. The last time was in 1986." (Whether that was to exorcise the diamond demons responsible for that year's World Series loss to the Mets is uncertain.) Sometimes, the sod reappears in strange, if appropriate places. Carl Yastrzemski once used it to adorn his lawn in Lynnfield, Massachusetts, perhaps the ultimate example of taking your work home with you.

In actual fact, the original Fenway grass preceded even the park which houses it. When Fenway was first built in 1912, the team had brought the actual turf with it from their previous park, the Huntington Avenue Grounds. The late Captain Ellery Clark, author and historian, suggested that as a result, "There appeared to be both a spiritual and a physical connection between the old and new parks."

During the off-season, Mooney maintains a small crew to replace seats, carry out general painting and maintenance, and order supplies for the forthcoming year. During the course of a year, the number of crew members fluctuates from a half dozen to as many as thirty or forty.

Mooney's crew is highly motivated and extremely dedicated. They seem to realize that theirs is more than a maintenance job, that they have been en-

The Grounds

"It's the only ball park when with one out and a man on first, when a ground ball is hit to the shortstop, over my earphones I get this hum of anticipation from the fans that this is a double play ball. I don't get that in any other park."
— Ken Coleman

Mooney is an "armchair general," Forester adds: "Joe comes along with his rake and gives it a level job. After that the kid comes along and puts a cocoa mat on it, which is just like a doormat you see in front of a home. It's made out of rope. And he'll take that and smooth it all out, and then another kid will come along with a roll, a light roll, and

trusted with preserving a national treasure. Veteran Al Forester joined the crew back in 1957 and speaks proudly of his labors, and the contribution he makes to Red Sox baseball. "During the games I'm stationed down at what we call 'canvas alley.' It's a box seat, first row. We're down there for two things: in case something happens on the field, and for the fifth-inning drag. Other than that, anytime it rains we all run out and get the canvas down. Every time you put it on, it gets heavier and heavier. I might be one of the senior members but we're all grounds crew, we're all equal. We all have to push that tarp out.

"The infield is the main thing. That's where the bounces are. You don't get that many bad bounces off of grass. The dirt is maybe two feet [deep] in some places, three in others. If I see a bad hop during the game, I blame it on the infielders, because they often fail to smooth over the divots they themselves cut with their spikes. Bad hops don't

come from pebbles. That's all DIRT out there, screened dirt with a mixture of loam, sand, and clay. After the game is over, we have two fellas go out with this aluminum drag. It fills in all the divots. The following morning when I come to work I put some water on to wet the infield and all the dirt along first and third. After it's wet I take an infield pull machine, like a sand-trap machine they use at golf courses. I bring out what we call a nail drag—it's got three hundred nails on it—and attach it to the back end and just drag that thing, make like a figure eight, up and back, working my way from first to third. Then I'll go the long way, back and forth, till I got it all scratched up. And now we've got a little cushion out there."

And in case there was any notion that

70

Fenway Saved

roll it, put the water on it, and we're all set to go.

"The mound dirt is altogether different. That's all red clay from New Jersey, from about the position of the pitcher when he starts his delivery, about two feet in back of the rubber, down to about nine feet in front. He wants something *solid* for his follow-through. Eventually he'll make a hole there but it's not going to be a big hole. But if you put in the same dirt as you have on the infield, no way. You wouldn't last four innings in a ball game. Eventually they might say to get out there, the hole is too big for the Red Sox pitcher. You go out with a rake and a pounder and scratch it up, fill it back in and just pound it down."

Some of the tasks might entitle the crew to hazardous duty pay. "Sometimes I even go up on The Wall in left and get those balls up there in the net. You can't let just anybody go up there. You only have so much time to get up there and get down before the ballplayers come out to play the game. If a kid goes up there and he's frightened, now it's going to take maybe half an hour to get him down."

Although Mooney and his crew have maintained the grounds immaculately for decades, Billy Rogell, who played for the Red Sox back in the 1920s, recalls a distinctly less pampered field. "Today in the fifth inning, they go out and they all clean up the infield. I used to pick up stones. A half a pocket full of stones, when I played shortstop. Detroit, Bos-

ton, all the rest of them, because those small stones, they'd come up. I'd pick them up and put them in my back pocket. By the time the ballgame was over, I'd have a half a pound, a pocketful of stones.

"Oh, they keep the grounds good today. Today, they cut the grass, but in certain parks, I don't think they cut it as good as they used to. After all, if it's their home ground and the manager tells them to

The Grounds

do this or do that, the grounds people have to do it. And of course, if you've got big grass—ground balls, it slows them up. If it's cut close, that ball goes through there like a bullet."

Doctoring the field has been a tradition at certain parks, and one can't say that the Red Sox have not themselves engaged in the practice. Certainly Mooney is such a forceful personality that one half wonders if Sox management could convince him to do anything he doesn't want to do. Inevitably, pitchers and hitters hold differing views on the subject. Jim Lonborg, Cy Young award winning pitcher for the 1967 Impossible Dream team, does recall some tailoring.

"Sure, we'd try to influence shaping the field. Letting the grass grow a little bit longer in the infield. If the hitters were going to get an advantage with The Wall, the pitchers have to get an advantage somewhere. So we'd try to get the grounds crew to let the grass grow longer, and then the hitters would complain about how they couldn't hit a ball through the infield.

"It was more from a defensive standpoint. If your pitcher is pitching and he's giving up ground balls, and they're slowed down by the height of the infield grass, there's more of an opportunity for your defensive team to get the hitters out. That kind of went off and on over the years while I was there.

"At one point, when they cut the grass too short, we'd have them water it down heavily in front of home plate, to dampen the earth and kill the ball. We always tried to get some kind of a compromise with our hitters that would be beneficial to our pitching staff, and which hopefully would be beneficial to the team.

"If you knew some teams were coming in, and they had some guys that were great bunters, they could make arrangements to do things with the field, to grade the foul lines a bit so that a ball right down the line might tend to run foul. People weren't interested in bunting at Fenway."

Despite considerable evidence to the contrary, Mooney discounts the notion that tailoring the park can help the home team. "There's not a groundskeeper on earth that won any games for anybody. The field actually has nothing to do with

the ball game… It's the same thing with guys you see bless themselves before they bat. The guy on the mound, he could be a Catholic, too. What if they *both* bless themselves?"

Regardless of such ethical and religious nuances, Fenway's field has a well-earned reputation throughout baseball. George Higgins indicates, "Fenway was always considered a premier playing surface.

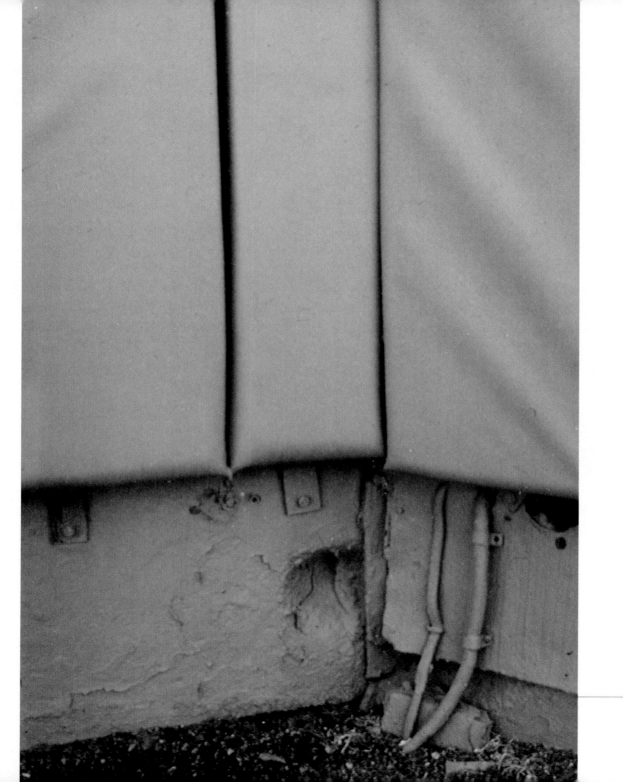

Fenway's impeccable infield is mowed vertically and horizontally, and short, so that nubbed infield hits will get to Sox infielders faster than fleet opponents can make it to first base. The outfield is mowed in concentric semicircles and also coifed for ball speed."

Mooney takes his work dead seriously, but at the same time minimizes any attempts to glorify his task. "It don't take an Einstein to put bolts into concrete and break out concrete with a jackhammer. The guy who works here the longest is on the mound, Jim McCarthy. Forty-something years. He does the mound and home plate, and the watering when the team's on the road. During the game I do everything. I walk the stadium, check and see if the rest rooms are all right, check for broken water pipes. This and that. Anything. The easy days are a lot more common than the hard days. The crew don't tell you about when they just come in and sit around all day doing nothing.

"The field is Merion bluegrass, which is a good grass for this part of the country all the way down to southern Pennsylvania, Maryland; below that you might move into Bermuda. Various spots get work and re-sod during the year… Bluegrass grows dormant in the winter; it's often under snow, ice, whatever. You're in New England, remember.

"The infield and outfield are a sandy soil mixed with Turface, which we cut in two or three times a year. Otherwise, just good topsoil everywhere. Anytime the team goes on the road we re-level the

Fenway Saved

The Grounds

dirt of part the infield, especially at the edge of the infield and outfield grass, otherwise they get a lip. We cut the grass every day. It's an inch in the infield. And the clay around the plate and on the mound has to be good.

"Ninety percent of our people think, 'Oh gee, you're off all the time, the whole winter. You've got a hell of a job.' They think we have like government jobs where we don't work half the time and they have to support us. They don't know all the big maintenance jobs are off-season. This park's always been well maintained. The Red Sox have always spent money to keep it up and keep it clean."

Carl Yastrzemski credits Mooney with ex-

ceptional care. "I've always thought it's the best field in baseball. I didn't have to worry about a bad hop, so I could charge balls and take chances, knowing I'd always get a true bounce. If there was a spot out in the field that wasn't quite right, especially in the dirt part past the foul line, I'd ask Joe Mooney to come out and he'd pound it down by hand. Joe was in charge of the park's maintenance and he took exquisite care."

Perhaps Mooney's predecessor was not quite so punctilious. Ted Williams was a focused student of virtually every aspect of the game. In his second stint of military service, flying combat missions with John Glenn over Korean during the Korean War, Ted missed the entire 1952 season and most of the 1953 season. Despite having been away from Fenway Park for nearly two years, the first time he took batting practice at Fenway, starting to get ready to get back in condition, he noticed that home plate was out of alignment, and called over Joe Cronin. "Hey, Joe, what the hell have you done to this plate while I was gone?" Williams roared. "It's out of line." It was already mid-season and Cronin couldn't believe it, but Ted insisted, and they finally checked. In fact, it was off by a fraction of an inch, something no one else had noticed.

Yankee Stadium may have a well-deserved reputation as the Bronx Zoo, but real wildlife has always presented challenges to Fenway Park. George Sullivan comments at length on the pigeon. "The pigeon is Fenway Park's national bird," journalist Harold Kaese once suggested. Pigeons have played a memorable role in the history of Fenway, where they once abounded in the eaves of the grandstand roof. They have changed the course of games. They have gotten Ted Williams in trouble. And they have soiled the clothing of more than one customer, which some contend is a good-luck sign."

However, pigeons didn't help the Red Sox luck on at least two occasions in 1945. One got in the way of Hal Peck's throw after the Athletics outfielder had chased down Skeeter Newsome's hit in the right field corner. There are two versions of what happened next. One is that the throw was wild and, after striking the bird, the ball deflected into the hands of the second baseman who tagged out Newsome. The other says Newsome was safe.

In another game with the A's that season, Sox center fielder Tom McBride chased a pigeon he mistook for Sam Chapman's line drive.

Pigeons have gotten in the way of batted baseballs, too. Shortstop Billy Hunter of the Browns nailed one during batting practice in 1953. The bird plunged to the Fenway outfield, shook out the cobwebs, looked around, then took off. Willie Horton apparently mortally wounded a pigeon with a sky-high foul pop in 1974. The bird was carted off by a groundskeeper and put in the runway next to the Tiger bench for disposal after the game. But when the groundskeeper returned, the pigeon was gone.

Scores of other pigeons couldn't walk away. Considered nuisances, they were shot in the wing by Ted Williams, who'd take up residence in one of the bullpens with a rifle and pick off 50, 60 or 70 at one sitting. Sometimes he was joined by Tom Yawkey.

The Grounds

One can imagine Mooney's reaction in the early 1980s, when Baltimore came to play on a rainy Sunday afternoon. After play was halted and the tarp laid down, it soon filled up with rainwater. Rick Dempsy, the O's catcher, charged out of the dugout, his uniform stuffed with towels like an overblown team mascot, and strode to the plate. He then pantomimed Babe Ruth's "Called Shot", connected on the phantom delivery, and proceeded to run the bases, belly-flopping head first into each of the bases and ending in a headfirst slide home to the cheers of the spectators. The TV-38 cameras captured the event. While bringing much hilarity to viewers, Joe Mooney's perspective on the event was totally different to this protector of Fenway, it was not funny. You don't treat Mr. Mooney's property so lightly. Dempsey ripped the tarp with his spikes; the Orioles recieved a rebuke and a hefty bill for damages. Dempsey was eventually traded.

Mooney probably wasn't too pleased, either, when Roger Clemens—celebrating the Sox winning the pennant in 1986—jumped on the back of a State Police horse and rode around the field whooping it up.

It was a rat which prompted one of the greatest moments of baseball footage ever caught on camera. The story is told by NBC-TV director Harry Coyle of how cameraman Lou Gerard, working from inside The Wall got the shot of Red Sox catcher Carlton Fisk waving & leaping, his body language willing his long drive fair during that famous sixth game of the 1975 World Series. "It was an historic picture, and people don't realize how close it came to the trash can. Fisk was up to bat, and Lou was focusing the camera on him when, all of a sudden, he noticed something about four feet away from him—a rat....Yep, right there next to him. But that's OK—the rat helped make the shot. See, Lou had one eye on the rat and one on the camera—he was preoccupied, you can imagine—so when Fisk hit the ball, Gerard didn't dare go through the movements needed to shift the viewfinder and follow the ball. He played it nice and safe and stationary—he kept the lens on Fisk. Who knows, if the rat hadn't showed up for a guest appearance, it's possible Lou would have switched to the ball, even with the mist. And we'd have missed the shot which really changed TV sports coverage around...since then we've had a ton of Reaction shots."
– Curt Smith, Voices of the Game

Probably the primary reason that Fenway Park has been kept so well over the years is that for Tom and Jean Yawkey, it was like home, albeit a home with one hell of a backyard. Jean Yawkey remembered, "I told him [Tom] we should have an apartment here because we spend so much time here. We used to take a blanket and spread it out in the outfield. We had a radio and a snack and listened to the game, in the sun, looking for four-leaf clovers too, to try to win the game.

"When I think of the ballpark I think of Tom. He knew everybody in this ballpark. He had a nickname for everybody who worked here—his own nickname. He loved this place. He never would have been happy in another ballpark."

AROUND THE PARK

"Good afternoon ladies and gentlemen, boys and girls, and welcome to Fenway Park for today's game between the Baltimore Orioles and the Boston Red Sox. . . and now here are the starting lineups for today's game."

With this simple but elegant greeting, Sherm Feller, Red Sox public announcer from 1967 through 1993, opened countless games at Fenway Park, changing only the name of the visiting team. These words represent the formal welcome to Fenway, the beginning of an experience that many will never forget. For many, the first trip to this park is one of life's rites of passage—as important as the first kiss.

As you stroll around the circumference of Fenway Park, making five turns rather than the customary four it takes to circle a normal block, if you look beyond the ravages of age, you will notice that the park's crusty exterior still shows signs of its formidable regality of yesteryear.

Much of the park's splendor has aged into a graceful decline. The cracks and graying brick provide a discourse on the battering it has taken from the harsh New England elements. Remarkably, Fenway has survived nearly 100 years and may reach the full century mark before it is closing time for this fabled Red Sox home.

Fenway's bricks need re-pointing, unused windows of a bygone era are bricked up, yet they somehow add lustre and charm reminiscent of the ancient days of glory and grandeur, when Babe Ruth, Foxx, Runnels and Ted Willliams strode through the gates on Van Ness Street on their way to the clubhouse.

When attending a performance—for every game at this grand venue rises to that level—as you hasten to your gate of entry, you may not observe high up on the walls the intricate details indicating that this was not a cheap production. Fenway Park was built to endure, and endure it has without any of the slickum applied to the decade-newer Yankee Stadium.

As you wend your way toward the turnstiles—your momentum dictated by the crowd—take notice above you of the diamond motif around the facade on Yawkey Way, embroidered by a master bricklayer. Or you might try to catch a glimpse of a glorious geometric art deco capitol standing out against the brick, painted in one of the various greens that adorn the park, inside and out.

Bronze plaques honor Tom Yawkey, hinting of the storied franchise's history. A floral motif one story high at the corner of Brookline Avenue and Yawkey Way suggests another era when additions provided space for offices and now souvenir sales, and of course the exclusive Diamond Club.

As you approach the ramp up to the seats, with head down on a bee-line for your seat, you might just manage to spot the old Red Sox logo painted red, now worn and grounded into the cement pavement, more beautiful perhaps in its old age. Oh, the stories it could tell of her once radiant days.

Part of what could be called the Miracle of Fenway is not only the fact that around 30,000 people have managed to attend each game there over the past several years, but the journey of discovery inherent in getting there, in actually finding the place for the first time.

This adventure of sorts has been written about often, but never more effectively than by novelist W. P. Kinsella and former Bosox star Bill Lee.

FENWAY FIRSTS

Aside from all the history and romance, finding the park can be something of an adventure not unlike the fictional experiences depicted when W. P. Kinsella's character in the book Shoeless Joe, *on which the movie* Field of Dreams *is based, kidnaps reclusive author J. D. Salinger and brings him to Fenway Park:*

"A vision of what I have to do flashed in front of me as I heard the announcer's instructions: a scene that might have been projected by a shadow box was outlined on one of the clouds that hung over the stadium. The picture was of me and J. D. Salinger seated at Fenway Park in Boston watching a baseball game, our hands busy with hot dogs, soft drinks, and scorecards. The scene was in black and white…

"I am fortunate. Two tickets in Section 17. 'Right behind the Red Sox dugout,' the elderly ticket seller assures me; his right eye is sightless, rolled back, and what is visible looks like a mixture of milk and cherry blossoms…

"We hit Boston at the beginning of rush-hour traffic, and of course I become lost immediately. I travel over a number of bridges and drive along the ocean, trying all the while to weave in the general direc-

tion of the Prudential Building, which I know is in the vicinity of Fenway Park and is the one landmark in Boston that I know. But the traffic sweeps my Datsun along like a cork in a swift current, past corners where I want to turn, and I am carried onto and over expressways. I eventually work the car to an exit and return to the bunched streets. Quite by accident, we end up on a main street and I can see the silvery light standards of Fenway Park.

"I have to make a left turn. Pedestrians in the East…Cars bound together like tiny coupled trains stretch over a hill and beyond the baseball park. I picture myself being forced onto another expressway, and in an hour or so reappearing at this corner, only to be swept by again.

"Then suddenly, like the parting of the Red Sea, a parking place appears one row to my right 'More of a miracle to find a parking place on a baseball night in downtown Boston than for a man to throw away his artificial leg and grow a new one in front of an enraptured congregation,' I say to Salinger…

"I wait until we are settled in our seats at the stadium—good seats directly behind the Red Sox on-deck circle (although the seats are much too close together and we are hunched knees close to chins, as if we were passengers in the rear seat of a foreign car)—before attempting to discuss Salinger's life with him again…

"'I've come fifteen hundred miles to drag you to a baseball game….Look at that left field fence, half as high as the sky. The Green Monster. Think of the men who patrol that field, the shadow of that giant behind them, dwarfing them." It is ironic, I think, that the place chosen for me to bring Salinger has no left field bleachers, while in my own park I have only a left field bleacher.

"We stare at the feather-green field in silence…."

Fenway Saved

As a rookie just in from the Coast, Bill "Space-man" Lee also had his own particular problems with Boston geography. Navigating his car through narrow Boston streets toward an apparent mirage known as Fenway Park, when he was first asked to report to the big league club, Lee found it a bit hard to locate Fenway. "I had never seen Boston or Fenway Park. Driving down the turnpike into Boston, I caught my first glimpse of the lights of Fenway and of its notorious left field Wall, the Green Monster. The stadium was so close to the highway you could almost touch it as you rode by. A sign warned me that the next exit was about two hundred fifty yards ahead to the right. I figured, Great. All I have to do is get off here and cut back to the ballpark. No problem....

"[I found I had] gone to hell without realizing it. I was condemned to drive an eternal highway that would only bring me past the ballpark without ever letting me enter its gates. I kept looking in the rear view mirror, expecting to find out I had just crossed over into the Twilight Zone. Just as I was about to panic I got hold of myself and adapted. Deciding that this was a foreign environment and that the only way to conquer it was to submit to it, I humbled myself in surrender to the Boston topography and became caught in its spiritual flow. I also stopped and asked for directions."

Carl Yastrzemski recalls walking into Fenway for the first time after being signed: "I still remember little things about that moment: the huge board shaped like a baseball. It had holes in it with a player's name over each one, and asked fans to contribute to the Jimmy Fund. Each donation a fan made was in the name of a favorite player. I imagined what it would be like to have my name on that big ball. The Jimmy Fund, for children's cancer research, Mr. Yawkey's baby. Until a new scoreboard was erected in the 1970s—with advertising—the Jimmy Fund sign was the only one that Mr. Yawkey allowed in the park. It was a huge billboard over the right field stands."

The job of welcoming fans to Fenway and introducing the players has evolved over the years. In the early years, before the park had loud speakers, the team had men with megaphones and booming voices, including one Wolfie Jacobs, roam the stands announcing the players. Perhaps the most memorable voice of Fenway Park, however, was Sherm Feller, whose reserved but dulcet tone spoke volumes to generations of Red Sox fans.

Sherm Feller was a hard act to top (even though he once entered a "Sherm Feller sound-alike" contest run by a local radio station—and lost!) He once told an interviewer, Mike Bryan, "They don't want me to be a star here, and I don't want to be. I just want to enjoy the game and inform the public. The baseball fan in Boston is much more discriminating than the fan anywhere else. The other team gets as much applause as the home team for a great play. They're very conservative here. No Chesterfield signs on the walls. No signs at all on the left field Wall. The old man (Tom Yawkey) gave in to the other ads very

Much goes on behind the scenes at Fenway—in the clubhouse, the press box, and the executive offices, and in the stands.

Before the game, the concession people (Harry M. Stevens for decades, Aramark today) prepare the food and ready themselves for the game. Outside in the streets, vendors put sausages on the grill, or arrange their other various wares. Outside Gate A, Nicky Jacobs sets up his wooden peanut pushcart—the same one his father George used for 44 straight years before him, and his father's father before that. Nicky claims that the family has sold peanuts outside Gate A since Fenway first opened in 1912. His dad used to love to take the customer's money, then toss the paper-wrapped bag of peanuts in such a way that almost every one would fumble and drop it. When he died in 1988, Sharon Lynch of the Associated Press reported that Fenway fell silent for a moment in his honor. If they do this for a peanut vendor, whatever will they do for Ted?

reluctantly. Somebody talked him into it. He would have preferred all-green walls, I'm sure.

"The first night a team's in town, I've got to get in maybe ten minutes earlier to learn the names. The players get very upset if you don't pronounce their names right. How would you say D-e-v-o-n White? Well, I said DE-von first. Then I found out. The ballplayers get mad at me when I say 'Error!' too loud. 'Don't you think they know I made an error?' Rick Burleson said to me after I'd said, 'Er-ror, second baseman.' He hated it. I don't blame him. If I like the guy, I might make believe the mike doesn't work. I've got power up here, I suppose. With Yaz I never said his name, just 'Number Eight.' It didn't matter what I said anyhow. They'd drown me out. Almost the same with Boggs. They drown me out. He likes it. He doesn't say anything to me but I know he likes it. I'm a show person and I know what they like."

Jim Perry sells sunglasses—even after night games ("Get your Nomar sunglasses! Mo Vaughn sunglasses!") On fine summer weekends, retired Boston police deputy chief Ed Walsh sets up a couple of tables of baseball cards. "I used to get John-Henry Williams [Ted's son] into Fenway all the time. They didn't know him. 'What the hell,' I said, 'his father built the place.'"

Inside the park, the players have arrived and begun their pre-game routines. This is the same locker room used by all the greats. As described by John Hough, "There is no cop at the green door that leads to the Red Sox clubhouse. When you knock, the door is opened. To your right, a narrow corridor leads to the manager's office…A second door, unguarded, admits you to the clubhouse.…They all came down this tunnel. Tris Speaker, Smoky Joe Wood, Babe Ruth, Joe Cronin… The dugout is as simple as can be. You step up to the bench. Now and then a mouse can be seen tightroping on one of the electric wires draped along the back wall…"

Former Red Sox first baseman Mo Vaughn described his pre-game ritual: "I've got the messiest locker in the entire world. Inside, I've got pictures of places I've been, cards, and photographs of myself with my favorite players. I keep pens, pieces of paper, books, spikes—anything that has been given to me. I've got T-shirts in there that I've had since college! They're all lined up, and even though I might not use them, it's important for me that they be there. All of the things in my locker are like a diary of everything I've done."

Vaughn stresses relaxation before a game, keeping his mind clear and his body loose. He wears old, loose clothing during his workout and batting practice, then takes a shower afterwards. He follows a ritual of getting taped and dressed. His ankles and wrists are taped to prevent injury from sprains.

Many players have invariable—almost sacred—routines to which they adhere before and during the game. Wade Boggs was known for only eating chicken on game days. He also followed a habit of deliberately stepping over the first base line going onto the field, and stepping on it as he left his position, or was it the other way around? It only took a few times watching Nomar Garciaparra at bat before people noticed his constant ritual tightening of the batting gloves and fans began counting the number of times he tapped his toes as he waited for the pitcher to get ready to throw. Like some exotic, highly-strung bird, Garciaparra also re-enters the dugout from the field each time with a very specific, deliberate step.

GONE WITH THE WIND

One of the other, somewhat more scientific things Mo Vaughn did was to check the weather carefully each day. Dom DiMaggio always checked the prevailing wind.

"You knew the wind in your own park. When I saw the flag blowing in, over The Wall, I went to the opposite field. A player who wasn't there all the time wouldn't know the ball'd just hang up there

if he hit it into that wind. The Wall keeps beckoning, and you really need someone on your ball club that knows what it's like." Yaz checked the wind, too. He called it an obsession. He would check the weather first thing when he got up in the morning, catch every report he could, and then, once at the park, before he even went into the clubhouse he'd go into the stands to see which way the wind was blowing. Then as he dressed at his locker, he could begin making the necessary mental adjustments as he suited up.

The players take batting practice, Red Sox first, then the visitors. Out by Pesky's Pole, a clutch of fans stands near the rail hoping for a ball—fair or foul, or on a hop—to enter the stands for a ready

souvenir. Others cluster near the Red Sox dugout hoping for an autograph. Dwight Evans, to name just one, would put on a bit of a show for the opposition as he went through his workout in right field. He would practice his throws from right with intensity—to make an impression on the opposing team watching him in the field. It might give him an edge; they might be less likely to test his arm. Sometimes defense can be improved on reputation alone. The plays that aren't made can be nearly as important as those which are. Boggs worked hard on improving his fielding, and he would often take as many as 100 ground balls a day, to work on his fielding at third, where others took maybe a dozen.

In earlier days, Tom Yawkey would sometimes come early. Carl Yastrzemski talks about how Yawkey kept a locker next to his. "All he ever hung in it was his sweater, a beige sleeveless sweater that was as plain as he was. No player ever took that locker. He wanted it open so he could sit next to me and talk." Yawkey used to like to take his own batting practice when the park was deserted. "He hit right handed and his dream—after winning a World Series, which we never did—was to hit a ball off The Wall." He never did that, either. He liked to hit it into the stands, though, and would bring the batter's box right next to the seats.

Dennis Liborio, a former Sox batboy, also recalled how Yawkey would take batting practice. "Mr Yawkey worked out on the field every day with us. A guy would hit pepper at us from home plate and we'd line up at the screen. I'd protect Mr. Yawkey

Fenway Saved

to the right of him, Vince Orlando to the left of him, and another kid to the left of Vinnie. Mr. Yawkey had a Ty Cobb model glove about the size of his hand. We'd get to the ballpark between ten and eleven, but sometimes it would be after three before he'd get down to the field for his pepper game. Then every month he'd give us fifty to a hundred dollars for playing with him."

When batting practice is done, the batting cage is folded up and rolled around the field and back under the stands, and the grounds crew finalizes preparation of the infield, the mound and around the plate. John Updike, attending Ted Williams' last game, described watching a groundskeeper "treading the top of this wall, picking batting-practice home runs out of the screen, like a mushroom gatherer seen in Wordsworthian perspective on the verge of a cliff."

The player's world is really their own. The fans approach the park in a wholly different manner, many taking the subway to Kenmore or engaging in various parking strategies and then hoofing it over. It is this coming to the park, walking through the streets towards to the park in anticipation of the game which is an important part of the experience for most Red Sox fans. Many have felt the emotions heighten with the first glance of the light standards, and the scalpers buying and selling tickets, the buzz of the crowds as they converged from all sides. Roger Angell talks about a sense of belonging that can develop. In 1967 as the Red Sox moved toward a pennant which seemed impossible when the season began, people all over New England were caught up in the story.

"Late in August, a patient recovering from surgery stood at the window of his room in the New England Baptist Hospital night after night, watching the lights of Fenway Park across the city and hearing the sudden double roar of the crowd—first over his radio and then, in a deep echo, through the warm night air. The sense of belonging was best in the crowded streets near the ballpark before game time. Up out of the subway on Commonwealth Avenue, up Brookline Avenue and over the expressway bridge, past the Pennant Grille, past the button-hawkers 'Go, Sox!') and the ice-cream wagons and the police horses; carried along in a mass of children and parents, old ladies in straw porkpies, pretty girls with pennants, South Boston and Dorchester youths in highschool windbreakers, a party of nuns; then pushed and jammed, laughing at the crush, through the turnstiles and into the damp gloom under the stands; and out at last to that first electric glimpse of green outfield and white bases—this is the way baseball is remembered, and the way it truly was, for once, in the summer of the Red Sox."

Things have changed over time. Bill Lee: "Fans always come to the ball park because it's in close proximity to the working people. It's structured so you can get off work, get a pizza and a beer and watch a good ball game. And before it got so media dominated, the games would start at 7:30 and be over at 9:00. You'd be home with your wife by

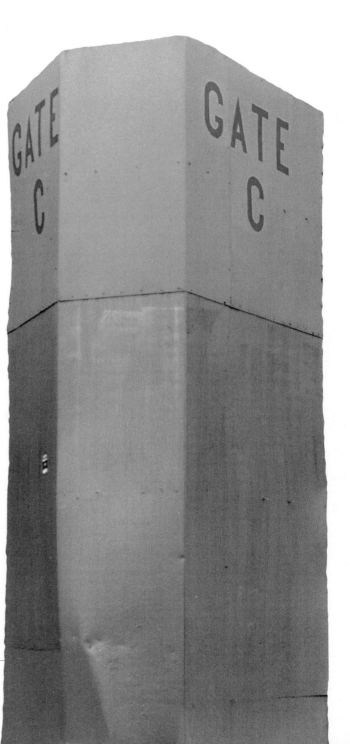

Around the Park

10 o'clock. Now it's gotten so media oriented, it's changing the lifestyles of the fans." Games now last longer, but the team has experimented with different starting times with considerable success.

The media people would arrive as per their own schedules. There haven't always been good press box or broadcast facilities at Fenway. In fact, as late as 1950, there was no broadcast booth at all. Vin Scully's first network broadcast was of a football game at Fenway, with Harry Agganis playing, and since there was no booth, he had to broadcast from the roof. He had not brought a coat with him and had "only a 60-watt bulb, his mike and 60 yards of cable." It was freezing. He later got a letter of apology from the Red Sox, and changes were effected.

BATBOYS, BOO-BIRDS & OBSTRUCTED VIEWS

Pesky's Pole, the tall yellow foul pole which marks the dividing line between fair and foul territory down the right field line, is another one of those quirks that endear Fenway Park to its fans.

Johnny Pesky explains the origins of this feature which bears his name: "When Mel Parnell was here working with Coleman and Martin, broadcasting, there was a ball hit down the right field line, and I guess it won a ball game. Parnell comes on as the jock and he says, 'Johnny hit a few home runs down

there. As a matter of fact, he hit a home run to win a ball game for me.' That's how that name began. They started calling it Pesky's Pole. I don't know how long they're going to keep doing that. It's very flattering.

In fact, it's only 302 feet right down the line in right, but few home runs ever go out there because The Wall goes so sharply backwards that the average distance in right is 382 feet. Both in right and left, the crowd is close to the playing field. There has always been a lot of interaction between players and fans at Fenway, and maybe it's more intense simply because of the proximity between the two. Former Red Sox reliever Bob Stanley says, "It starts before the game. I'm down in the bullpen warmin' up, they're yellin' at me. They're booin'. This one guy was screamin' at me. *Screamin'*. You guys wouldn't believe what I hear in the bull pen sometimes."

Fans do affect the action once in a while, reaching over to try and snare a ball hit towards the stands, but this kind of interference is actually rare. Once upon a time, however, John Donovan, Red Sox Executive Vice-President and Counsel, did interfere. It was when he was a ballboy, as he was for three years before rising further in the ranks. "One day I'll never forget was against the Browns, I was working down the right field line. Williams hit a liner that I gloved on one hop and threw to Dick Kokos at second base. It was a fair ball. Umpire Cal Hubbard called me out from a corner of the dugout to tell me to pay attention, but Manager Joe McCarthy just said, 'Don't let it bother you.'"

Fenway hecklers riled Jackie Jensen so much that it took Mel Parnell and coach Paul Schreiber to hold him back from climbing into the stands after one in particular, back in 1956. Ted Williams' most famous spitting incident occurred at Fenway's largest single-game crowd ever (36,350). The Sox won the game on 1-0 on bases loaded walk to Ted in the 11th. Williams got along fine with fans when he played right field in his rookie year, 1939, but when he moved to left and the fans were looming over him, the press begin to pry into his family life, and it became too much. A lot of people get perverse pleasure out of taunting those they envy—from a distance—and Williams couldn't seem to let it roll off his back, so in a way he encouraged them further.

Jimmy Piersall, Mark "the Bird" Fidrych, Dennis "Oil Can" Boyd—there have been many colorful personalities at Fenway over the years, and the fans reacted to them in different ways. Yastrzemski wasn't particularly colorful, but he commented on the interaction with the fans: "…out in left, where they were so close, when they cheered it sounded fifty times louder. And when they got on you, it was so magnified that you thought the whole city of Boston was after you…No matter how crummy the team was, if you had only two thousand people in Fenway, that corner in left field would always be filled. It stuck like a ship's prow along the foul line. They were alongside you and right above you, so they could always shout down to you. Hide? It was the

worst thing you could think of doing. Because you couldn't hide, no matter how badly you messed up a play in the field or how terrible you had looked at the plate. Actually, I liked to listen to them. Some guy would get on me, and another fan would yell, 'Don't listen to him, Yaz. He's a jerk!' The next thing you knew, a fight would break out. My protectors against my detractors."

Yaz wisely turned the crowd interaction in his favor by using it for energy, and occasionally playing along. On one occasion, he came out with huge wads of cotton in his ears. "I would stand on first and look around, and you were so close that you could actually see the people. I don't mean the CROWD, but see the individuals and their features. It made it more personal, playing for each person, not just some big crowd. I guess I never stopped being psyched in this ballpark."

Williams, too, may have used the controversies he stimulated to good effect. Ed Linn suggests that these flareups seemed to occur when Ted got mired in a bit of a slump, that the feuds with press or fans fired Ted up, that it was quite possibly a technique he employed to get the juices flowing.

Needless to say, from time to time (less so since the club stopped selling beer after the seventh inning), fans would in fact venture onto the field, only to be ejected from Fenway Park, subject to arrest and prosecution. At other times, those in the seats have littered the field with a vast array of objects. On Caddy Day, hundreds of caddies tossed golf balls onto the field, delaying the game. Later, on Seat Cushion Night, with the Sox losing big, scores upon scores of seat cushions were sailed onto the field, also bringing about delay and a stiff warning about forfeiting a game that was destined to be lost in any event. There have been no more Seat Cushion Nights since.

At least some of the fans, those behind home plate, are restrained and protected by the screen. The metal screen behind home plate was the first of its kind in the major leagues. For decades, when a ball was fouled up on the screen and then began to roll down the sloping screen back toward the playing field, fans would accompany its progress with a "wooooOOOOP" rising in crescendo as the ball reached the lip and then came off the screen, into the hands of the waiting batboy. Woe be the batboy who dropped the ball. "Whenever I'd run out to catch a foul ball off the screen as the ball came rolling down," recalls Dennis Liborio, "if I missed it, they'd boo, but if I caught it there'd be silence. I'd always look up to the box after making the catch and see Mr. Yawkey watching me. 'Well,' he'd say to me later, 'I see old stone-fingers is getting better.'"

Since the screen was replaced, apparently as a relatively unnoticed part of the 1988 renovation, the lip is higher and more or less half the balls get stuck at the lip instead of dropping down. With the seats so close to the field, Fenway fans have to be especially vigilant, guarding against line drive fouls into the seats, or even the occasional airborne bat. Balls fouled off the press box or the 600 Club plexiglass facade can carom into the multitude of grasping hands. Fans in the luxury boxes can either earn a good round of applause with a nice grab, or a lusty boo if they fumble one and let it tumble to the seats below. For some fans, distractions seem the highlight of the day at Fenway—going after a foul, taking part in the Wave or having the chance to bat a beachball around.

The screen can support some weight. Ted Williams once climbed it behind home plate to get a bat he threw up there. So did literally a dozen or more fans in the Impossible Dream year, 1967. The minute the team cliched the pennant, thousands of fans ran onto the field. It became a frightening situation, with fans ripping up handfuls of grass and stuffing this in their pockets for a souvenir, tearing the team signs and other bits off the scoreboard and even climbing the screen toward the press box. People in the radio booths were gesturing at them to get down, because of the danger, but the manic fans were oblivious. Since that time, the Red Sox have wisely deployed mounted policemen, having them make a preliminary appearance as a sort of visual caution around the 7th inning.

Len Barker once threw a pitch so hard and so wild that it sailed completely over the batter, the catcher, the umpire and almost the entire length of the screen. The entire park was stunned into silence and then, about three seconds later, burst out into spontaneous laughter.

Up on the roof sit a few thousand other fans, in skybox seats. It's another world up there, with wooden walkways leading here and there as though boardwalks over shallow water. The roof is encumbered with all sorts of ventilation equipment, elevator housings, and sports a couple of food and souvenir stands of its own. The place is tar-papered, with a wooden ramp and little iron railings like the deck of a ship. Wooden steps led to the press room and the media areas which were nothing more than old-fashioned countrified shacks with screen doors. Very rural New England.

From a hitter's viewpoint, Fenway is a very good park. Ted Williams credits the clean features and lack of distractions with making him a better hitter. "It was everything," Dom DiMaggio said. "The backgrounds had a lot to do with it. The fans in the triangle—section 34 and Section 35 of the bleachers, in center field—used to wear white shirts at Fenway, and you couldn't see the ball. Finally they started shutting off that area so it was just green. And you could see the ball better." They've opened it up again since DiMag retired; now there are two platforms for TV cameras at the apex of Section 34, but for most home games the rest of that section and Section 35 are occupied by customers." The triangle has alternated between being blocked off and filled with bleacher creatures. In Dom's day, it was kept clear. When Tony Conigliaro was with the team, the area became known as Conig's Corner. Later on, though, as attendance climbed and seats were at a premium, the area was routinely filled with patrons, and for several years in the early to mid 1990s, one could even buy a season ticket

there, as a loyal cluster of fans did. For the 1998 season, the triangle was again closed off and those season ticket holders were offered other locations.

Not many have ever hit a home run over the center field wall—The Wall behind the bleacher seats. Carl Yastrzemski did in 1970, in the years before the higher extension atop the old brick wall was installed.

From most seats, a fan can see almost the entire park, but Fenway fans are such ardent admirers that one can even find paeans to the obstructed view seats, arguing that they would be missed in a new park! Several thousand fans in left can't see any ball hit down into the corner, and a somewhat lesser number of fans along the first base side can't see a ball hit down into the right field corner. That was just the scenario in 1990, for the final game of the season. Tom Brunansky was playing right for the

Red Sox, and there were two outs in the top of the ninth. The Red Sox had the lead. If he recorded the putout, the Red Sox would secure the AL East title. It was one of those balls you just couldn't see from the first base side. If you were sitting there, you had to watch and gauge the crowd reaction of people who were in a position to see and then yourself react accordingly. One of the tricks a person learns watching games at Fenway. Of course, a second later, everyone would know, but there is a collective and individual wish to know just a half-second sooner: did he catch it? did the Sox just clinch?

Bruno made the play, but not only did a few thousand at Fenway hesitate in uncertainty. So did the television audience. Both Bruno and the ball disappeared from camera view behind the part of the grandstand that juts out. Worse, no reply showed whether or not he caught the ball because ESPN's six replay cameras were focused on the crowd. Fortunately, the umpires had no trouble making the call.

Fans must be ever vigilant at Fenway. At any time you could be in imminent danger of getting struck by a foul ball. Especially when there's a sudden commotion in the bleachers, security men running up the steps, and half the fans are craning their necks to see what's happening. Or when the pennant races heat up, and fans scan the scoreboard ever more vigilantly for scores of the closest rivals.

When the manual operator pulls down the pitcher's number for the Yankees, you know that he's probably given up a few runs, and a ripple of anticipation can run through the crowd. You're looking to see their opponent score big. When you hear an unexpected loud cheer from the crowd, your eyes dart to the scoreboard to puzzle out what's just occurred. Tom Boswell remembers a game in which Toronto outfielder Sam Ewing darted in the door and posted a fictitious "8" next to the name of the Yankees' opponent.

AFTER IT'S OVER

After the game, the players grab their gear and leave the dugout. It's littered with sunflower seeds and empty Gatorade cups. It's not a pleasant sight. Nor are the stands. After a night game, the lights go down low and the cleaning crew comes out with big noisy blowers, driving the trash from under the seats and down to where it can be collected and removed.

Roger Angell could always be counted upon to paint the fullest picture, and the clubhouse has occasionally been a place for celebration. After the Red Sox won the pennant in 1967, he described the scene in the same book:

"The Boston locker room presented a classic autumn scene—shouts embraces, beer showers, shaving cream in the hair, television lights, statements to the press 'Never,' said Lonborg, 'do I remember a more…ecstatic and…vigorous moment..') … [The Sox had to wait for a later game's result, out of town, to know if they were tied for the pennant or had sole possession. When the Red

Sox heard that the Tigers had lost, and they had clinched] "every one of the Boston players came off the floor and straight up in the air together, like a ballet troupe. Players and coaches and reporters and relatives and even Yawkey and manager Williams hugged and shook hands and hugged again, and I saw Ricky Williams trying to push through the mob to get at his father. He was crying. He reached him at last and jumped into his arms and kissed him again and again; he could not stop kissing him. The champagne arrived in a giant barrel of ice, and for an instant I was disappointed with Mr. Yawkey when I saw that it was Great Western. But I had forgotten what pennant champagne is for. In two minutes, the clubhouse looked like a YMCA water-polo meet, and it was everybody into the pool.

"I visited both clubhouses, but I had seen enough champagne and emotion for one year, and I left quickly. Just before I went out to hunt for a cab, though, I ducked up one of the runways for a last look around Fenway Park, and discovered several thousand fans still sitting in the sloping stands around me. They sat there quietly, staring out through the half-darkness at the littered, empty field and the big wall and the bare flagpoles. They were mourning the Red Sox and the end of the great season."

John Hough captures the bittersweet mood after the last pitch has been thrown. "Half an hour after a game ends, the husky bouncer is still sitting by the door in the little hallway outside the clubhouse. I say good night; he nods and yanks the door open. Now the big concourse is empty. The tide has swept out, scattering hot dog wrappers, squashed paper cups, and a million tatters of peanut shell. The cement floor and painted brick walls breathe their stored-up smells of cigar smoke and beer. Somewhere a slatted metal door slams, sending echoes shuddering up and down the concourse."

One cannot underestimate the impact on the American mind of the image, whether derived from the Bible or the classics, of the contained green space. The force of such imagery may be the reason why some 45 million people a summer flow to baseball parks in the midst of the urban wilderness, flow in big cities to places which recall in some distant way the place that promised perfection, whose name we derive from the enclosed park of the Persian King, paradise.
— A. Bartlett Giamatti

FENWAY PARK AND THE AMERICAN CULTURAL LANDSCAPE

More than just another building, Fenway Park may be considered a "cultural landscape." One of the last survivors of the era of great ballparks built in the early twentieth century, it represents something far more important to us and our society than just an historic place where many great ballplayers once played. Whether we realize it consciously or not, the ballpark embodies a widespread attempt to harmonize competing cultural tensions (agrarian and industrial), while embodying the cultural values that were uniquely American.

101

As Matthew Bronski has written, Fenway and the other ballparks of its era "are common shared landscapes which evolved and acquired meaning over time. They are fusions of experience, location, landscape, technology, and aspirations which are bound up with time and memory. The field of play and the game itself objectify the ideals and emblems of an agrarian democracy and the cultivated green landscape through which it defined itself. The urban setting of the parks, and their industrial imagery of steel trusses, metal pipe railings, and silver light stanchions bring to mind the industrial forces that were brought to bear against the agrarian vision and drastically reshaped the American landscape. The rural ballpark was transformed and redefined by its insertion into the city fabric [and these ballparks] exist as part of a continuum of manifestations of American aspirations for a place where urbanity and industrial technology coexist in a profound way with agrarian virtue and pastoral innocence. These ballparks are among the most significant physical realizations of this deeply rooted America desire."

To the extent that Giamatti and Bronski are correct, this goes a long way toward explaining the deep emotional hold which parks such as Fenway have on the American psyche. It's not strictly rational, but rather operates at a far deeper level. It even explains why, among the newer parks, Camden Yards in Baltimore offers such immediate appeal (the pastoral green garden in an industrial city, represented by the warehouse just over the right field wall and the city skyline) while Chicago's new Comiskey Park does not. At the new Comiskey, there is too much open space around the stadium, with no shaping influence, for it to be seen in the urban context which would give it emotional force. The Ballpark at Arlington has lots of wonderful touches in the way of grillwork, columns, and quaint features, but it is set in the middle of a broad, featureless plain, isolated, like Comiskey, from the heart of the city.

Michael Gershman recalled his first trip to one of the classic old parks in *Diamonds:* "The first time I entered Ebbets Field I brought with me nothing but uncertainty. Walking through the tiled rotunda, uncertainty turned to curiosity. Emerging from a concrete runway, I experienced for the first time what W. P. Kinsella has knowingly called 'the thrill of the grass.' Seeing all that greenery, I felt at that moment as if I were in the land of Oz. When I walk into Fenway Park and Wrigley Field and Tiger Stadium, I still do."

Millions of people identify with that feeling, and many writers have attempted to express, sometimes rhapsodically, the first glimpse of greenness and the open expanse one enjoys upon emerging from a dark, enclosed concrete tunnel or ramp. It's clear that part of baseball's appeal has to do with images derived from pastoralism, agrarianism, innocence, openness and, now, nostalgia. Those who own Fenway Park are stewards of a facility which truly embodies these ideals; this is not a park which was created to try to capture the flavor of what once was—and people instinctively sense the difference between the original and a reproduction. This has an intrinsic value of its own, but it also is an asset which can be marketed effectively. The intimacy created by the closeness of the stands to the play-

ing field has great appeal. While the feeling might be recaptured for many of those seated in a new ballpark designed to look older, any attempt to replace a genuine ballpark with a reproduction or modern imitation meant to "feel authentic" may fall flat. It may in fact feel counterfeit, and lead instead to further disillusionment and disconnection.

Bronski surveys a swath of American cultural history and locates Fenway Park and the other ballparks of its era firmly within the great American dilemma: how to reconcile the Jeffersonian agrarian ideal with industrialization. Even Jefferson sought not pure wilderness, but a transformation of that wilderness into an Edenic garden. "Beginning in Jefferson's time, the cardinal image of American aspirations was rural landscape, a well ordered green garden magnified to continental size. This is the countryside of the old Republic, a chaste, uncomplicated land of rural virtue. In his remarkable book, *Virgin Land*, Henry Smith shows that down to the twentieth century the imagination of Americans was dominated by the idea of transforming the wild heartland into such a new 'Garden of the World.'"

Much of the greatness of America can arguably be traced to this attempt at melding these two impulses—to be rural and natural, and to be urban and industrial. Ralph Waldo Emerson "wished to see the physical city become more creatively related to its natural hinterland, and more internally 'natural' or 'organic.'" Interestingly, the land on which Fenway Park is built was first left undevel-

103

oped as part of the "Emerald Necklace" designed by great urban landscaper Frederick Law Olmsted. Olmsted deftly threaded the Emerald Necklace through Boston, one of America's oldest urban environments, just as he had placed Central Park within the denser urbanity of Manhattan. Lewis Mumford saw the American dichotomy, and therefore challenge, as that of the romantic personality and the utilitarian personality. For a long while in the nineteenth century, Mumford wrote, it looked as though the two might be able to exist harmoniously side by side. "Many of the leading minds—Audubon, F. L. Olmsted, Emerson, Marsh, Melville, Whitman, among others—could, with a wholeness of response, embrace the scientific and mechanical and the industrial and at the same time place these within the ample framework of man's natural and humanistic heritage."

Karl Marx and others in Europe elaborated the theory of socialism, in response to the overcrowded, hopeless onslaught of industrialism and urbanization. In America, by contrast, there was unsettled space on the continent providing ample room to expand. The frontier offered nearly unbounded possibilities for expansion without overcrowding.

Fenway and the other early 20th century ball parks were tailored to fit the sites on which they were constructed. "A crazy-quilt violation of city planning principles, an irregular pile of architecture, a menace to marketing consultants, Fenway Park works," according to Martin Nolan. " It works as a symbol of New England's pride, as a repository of evergreen hopes, as a tabernacle of lost innocence." That a park like Fenway could

be situated within these confines was a triumph. Fenway Park has always said something about community. "With the advent first of radio and then of television, the park became a sort of oversized town green for all New England," wrote Phil Patton in *Connoisseur*. It has also held an allure, an almost primitive, visceral hold on many in the same way migratory birds and salmon are held by the place from whence they come. The fans who are captured by the park's appeal return to Fenway as if by some homing instinct.

Most early ballparks were rural, and made for town play, not for a paying clientele. Hence the outfields were open, boundless, and encompassed the distant landscape beyond. This, and other features of the game, are part of the profoundly American allure of baseball, suggests Bronski. Not only is baseball the only major sport in America which is not run by the clock, and the only one which puts the focus on the quintessentially American values of individualism and self-reliance, it is also the only one which does not operate in a strictly confined space. Other team sports have a firmly defined rectangular playing field. Baseball offers a precise placement of the pitcher's mound, home plate, and the bases, but the two foul lines radiating out from home plate at precise angles extend theoretically forever.

Of course, these outfields were inevitably enclosed, particularly in the urban setting, for the very practical reason of limiting admission to paying customers. Thus,

"Whether you see Fenway Park or Wrigley Field as an Eden or not, you are out here because you remember something that you want revived."
— A. Bartlett Giamatti

A baseball diamond is meant to be an intimate stage scaled to a ritual as stylized as Kabuki: the viewers' focus is on two star players, encircled by a supporting chorus in special locations and roles; the stars face off and interact at center stage. The resulting visible movement is tight and fine-grained: a flashing ball, a catch, a throw, and one to three bodies running to points on the diamond 90 feet apart. Such dramatics are best witnessed in an intimate amphitheater that amplifies visual (and vocal) interaction—with bleachers low and tight around the action center—almost a part of it. Like Fenway.
— Benjamin & Jane Thompson,
Thompson Design Group

Bronski points out, the urban ballparks became a pastoral representation bounded within the city, much as Olmsted's Central Park, Prospect Park, and other urban parks created a representation of nature bounded within the city.

The physical setting of the park within the city creates unique characteristics. "The Wall," Bronski says, "is Fenway's concession to the odd plot on which it stands, a geometrical residue of rail yards and narrow streets and marshland." An odd feature like Duffy's Cliff had its purposes—extra paying spectators could be brought onto the field, increasing income for ownership. It also served as an early warning track. But Bronski suggests that there it represented more.

Many of the ballparks built both before and after the turn of the century incorporated earthen inclines such as Duffy's Cliff. The "shaping of a small hill at the perimeter of the outfield," suggests Bronski, "recalled the early notion of the outfield extending unbounded, encompassing the distant hills, valleys, and other topographic features." The Wall then, and today, is part of a "dialogue between the field and its urban site" which made such ballparks distinctive, but also offered more possibilities for the batted ball. The unpredictability which The Wall creates is one of its most loved features for the fans. The game is simply more interesting for the quirks created by some of the parks built in restricted spatial circumstances. As Bronski puts it, "the urban condition enriched the pastoral game."

It has even been suggested that the complex structure of the ballparks of this era leads perhaps to intellectual stimulus and that they serve as an aid to remembering specific events that occurred there. "In *The Art of Memory* Francis Yates relates how an architecture of specificity can serve as an aid to memory. The niches, the recesses, the spaces between columns, and the other secondary spaces of architecture can serve as a sort of 'honeycomb' in which the mind can store and associate specific people, things, or events to be remembered." Never underestimate the virtues—and even the importance—of a park such as Fenway to the intellect, at both the conscious and subconscious levels.

Fenway Park is one of the last of the parks which inherited and embodied these various sensibilities, and it's all the more precious for this reason. It offers a sense of comfort and home to people, sometimes unexpectedly. Doris Kearns Goodwin has written of growing up in Brooklyn and regularly attending games at Ebbets Field with her father. Ebbets was another one of the ballparks of Fenway's era, but was torn down and is still mourned by Brooklynites. Before her first trip to Fenway, Goodwin hadn't been to a ball park for many years. "I agreed," she wrote, "half reluctantly to go to Fenway Park. There it was again: the cozy ball field scaled to human dimensions so that every word of encouragement and every scornful yell could be heard on the field."

Fenway offers something special. It's not just another ball park, albeit an historic one. It really does inspire paeans to its virtue, partly because it's located in a city with a great literary and intellectual tradition and perhaps partly as well because of the subconscious appeal which Matthew Bronski has suggested. For countless reasons, many of which they can't analyze or describe, fans love Fenway. Perhaps that is why fans flock to Fenway year in and year out, even when the Red Sox are not contenders. It is a tribute to its success as a venue for baseball that the new generation of ballparks yearn to capture that which makes Fenway Park a truly extraordinary home for baseball.

One of the more unusual features of Fenway Park, unnoticed by many fans, is the subterranean Ryan Family Amusements found in the ballpark's basement (or, as they put it in their flyers, "Under Historic Fenway Park.") A member in good standing of the International Candlepin Bowling Association, the 20-lane candlepin bowling alley has been there "at least the 42 years I've been working here" according to the woman behind the desk. The complex, accessible from either Ted Williams Way or Yawkey Way and open twelve hours a day year-round, also houses eleven billiard tables and a score of video games.

On a bright and sunny spring day, while thousands of baseball fans cheer their boys of summer, downstairs in the smoky darkness, bowlers are seeking to record strikes of their own. Did someone record a strike at the exact moment that Roger Clemens struck out that 20th Mariner? Did someone throw a gutter-ball just as the ball went between Buckner's legs? Were billiard balls clacking as Ted Williams hit his final home run in September of 1960? Did Bill Lee ever play Space Invaders here?

Fenway is not the only interesting architecture in the Fens section of Boston. Fans rushing by, intent only on baseball, may ignore the intriguing building across the street. The Richardson Building, featuring a shield over its entrance, was named after PFC George Lincoln Richardson, who was killed near Verdun in 1918, and provides a formidable counterpoint to baseball. One wonders if George was perhaps grandson to H. H. Richardson, a major exponent of Romanticism in American architecture, whose finest building in Boston was Trinity Church. The elder Richardson worked with Frederick Law Olmsted at one point.

The Richardson Building's towering columns suggest solidity. Was this a house of finance in the Roaring Twenties, a place where Red Sox ownership might have banked the meager receipts of those most dismal of Red Sox teams? What has transpired in this structure over the years? Certainly in years past this grand facade has reflected more prosperous times. Commercial and cultural imperatives transformed the building into The Batter's Box, a cafeteria. Between the 1997 and 1998 seasons, it was converted to a souvenir stand.

LIVING AT FENWAY

by Bill Nowlin

Ball parks, and Fenway in particular, often evoke religious imagery from devotees. Even fans not given to such literary flights, or even to religion, find themselves making such comparisons. It's become commonplace to have Fenway described as a "shrine" by writers and commentators. Those who live at some distance from Boston speak of making the "pilgrimage" to this park. For myself, I can't remember a time when I wasn't making frequent visits to Fenway Park. For more than forty years I have "attended services" there on a reasonably regular basis. It's not a pilgrimage for me, since I go so often from my nearby Cambridge home. And whatever else you might say of the MBTA, it can never be mistaken for the road to Damascus. For me these trips are more akin to the weekly call to prayer.

109

At various intervals over recent years I have found myself at the park without any clear knowledge or recollection of the thought process or the emotional tug which brought me there. This mesmerism is less frequent now that I have season tickets, but the phenomenon does occur, even on game days when I've previously given away my own seats. Maybe it is just the ingrained habit of ritual, or perhaps it's that I had an unconscious need for a kind of spiritual refreshment.

Other times I'm there but I don't really want to be there. I began to experience this in my late forties. It's happened that I've awakened in maybe the 4th inning—

come back to my senses, my full faculties restored—and thought, "What am I doing here?" I occasionally find myself actually wanting to leave, to go home, but then I hesitate and inertia typically takes over. If I leave, something might happen and I'll miss it. Just another inning or two….

After all, there was that game in the late 1950s where the Sox were down 13-7 with two outs and nobody on in the bottom of the ninth. Just another meaningless game, in another meaningless season in a largely meaningless decade for Red Sox fans. The Sox, though, began to line single after single after single—not one walk

or double—and rallied to win the game. I could have missed it. It was exhilarating for those of the faithful who had stayed the course.

I still have a very strong and very inhibiting sense of guilt or shame if I even contemplate leaving early so, consequently, I hardly ever do. Even if moving to another seat, or going to the men's room in the latter innings, I don't want fans around me to notice and think I'm leaving. Should I actually leave before the final out, which I here admit I've done once or twice in recent years, I feel an urge to disguise myself, maybe hold up a folded newspaper to obscure my face like a Mafia boss leaving the courtroom. I speed up on the way out, walking purposefully, face angled downward to avoid eye contact, and only begin to relax when safely outside—beyond the imagined gazes of disapproval from more steadfast fans. Perhaps Fenway should have a confessional.

When I started going to Fenway in the late fifties, kids under 14 could ride the old MTA for a nickel, and they gave transfers from the bus to the subway and vice versa. I could ride my bike the mile and a half to Arlington Heights, take the half hour bus ride to Harvard Square, then go underground and make my way to Kenmore (back in the days before the lines were color-coded and this meant switching from the "Red Line" to the "Green Line"), all for five cents. A ticket to the bleachers was just fifty cents, and since I never ate or drank the ballpark fare, the whole day cost me under a dollar. Since I was pulling in the extravagant sum of two dollars a week from my paper route, I had it made.

The bleachers in those days didn't have any seats. The seating was simply on long planks. There were no seat backs or dividing lines. The individual seats came later, seemingly a section at a time, a sort of creeping Fenway gentrification. Likewise, some years later, the horse trough urinals in the men's rooms progressively disappeared, replaced with today's standard individual urinals. Where did they go? I've spoken with any number of male fans who regretted not claiming one for a backyard planter.

Late in the games, after the sixth inning or midway through the seventh, the usher guarding the gate between the bleachers and the grandstand would leave his post and you could cut through and take a better seat without paying the supplement. Given the poor attendance in those late Fifties/early Sixties games, when 8000 seemed an average draw, we had our choice of seats. Being typical, i.e., obnoxious kids, we liked to sit out in section 8, right behind a couple of crusty old-timers we'd spot puffing away on cheap cigars. Maybe only ten people were scattered in these section 8 seats, but we'd sit immediately behind these guys and start coughing and choking on the smoke. It's a wonder we never got thrown, or even punched, out.

During night games, the lights spotlighted a hazy cloud of smoke hovering over the field, drifting with the winds. All the seating areas in Fenway have

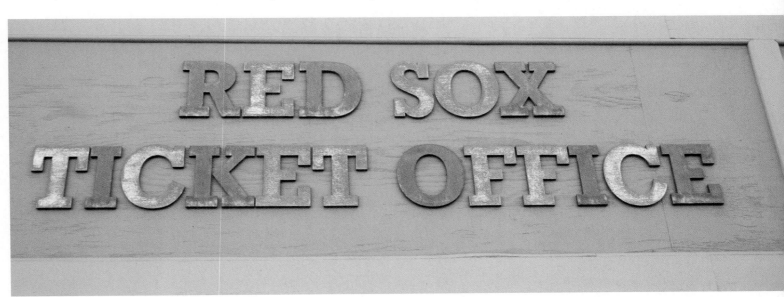

been smoke-free for a few years now, so you can now sit in your seat without suffering secondhand smoke. What this means, though, is that you must run a gauntlet under the stands where the smokers all puff away in clusters, filling up the unventilated tunnels with their exhalations.

There was no "Wave" in those days so the Bleacherites had to find other ways to entertain themselves. One day when the seats were about half-filled, I saw a woman pour a full beer all over her companion. This, needless to say, caused quite a stir. Then her friend walked down the steps, and back he came with a beer in each hand, proceeding to pour them over her, one after the other. More people began to notice. She left her seat and soon enough back she trudged with two beers of her own.

All over him, and now everyone had forgotten the game and was cheering them on as both of them walked down the steps together, disappeared under the stands and then emerged, each with two cups, walking all the way up to their seats—and then pouring them over each other once again. Now *that's* entertainment.

"There is only one person who could have hit it that far. Ted Williams. I could never reach that spot." – Mo Vaughn on the 502' home run hit by Ted Williams on June 9, 1946. The longest ever recorded at Fenway Park. This red seat, in a sea of blue seats, marks the spot where the ball landed.

As the Sixties progressed, and hippies brought peace and love to Fenway, there was a regular Bleacherite who sometimes bought all the ice creams from a vendor and threw them up one at a time into the seats to whoever could snag one.

More women began to come to Fenway. Maybe this had to do with the women's liberation movement and a certain freedom from prescribed gender roles. I've heard women suggest that maybe it had a bit more to do with player uniforms becoming not so baggy and a little more form-fitting. Morgana the Kissing Bandit was a feature for a while, running onto the field in many parks to kiss a player. In the bleachers, there was occasionally a female flasher down front who would turn around and pull up her shirt for the fans, perhaps a stripper from Boston's "Combat Zone" titillating the crowd with a sneak preview.

Later on, a meaner era prevailed and I recall inflatable sex-toy dolls being passed around, handled by boorish male fans in sloshed fraternity boy fashion. A certain ugly mob mentality surfaced. This sometimes occurred during "Reggie Sucks" chants and the like. Truly offensive, these dolls were banned and a stricter code of conduct began to be enforced in the park so that families would feel more comfortable and enjoy a relatively wholesome atmosphere. Pretty soon, the most excitement was watching Bob Stanley with a groundskeeper's rake pop beachballs that had strayed onto the field. Even before "Friendly Fenway" became a watchword, the powers that be made efforts to attract a wider array of people to the ball games. From a nearly exclusively male preserve, it is now not uncommon to find roughly half the crowd made up of female fans.

Fans began to speak up around this time, too, and complain about racist comments or foul language. The broadening ethnic composition of the team fortunately also led to, or coincided with, a commitment from the front office to diversify hiring throughout the organization and to actively welcome those who might previously have felt ex-

It was every kid's dream, when I was growing up. You come up to bat in the bottom of the ninth at Fenway, the Sox down 3-0, two outs, bases loaded. You step into the batter's box. Poised for greatness.

Well, it took about a half century before this rookie phenom made it. I signed up and sent in my contribution to the Jimmy Fund. I was given my check-in time, arrived, was issued my Red Sox shirt and suited up in the clubhouse. I stepped out onto the field and was walked out to the batting cages under the center field seats to work on my swing, my timing.

I was actually the first batter of the day, at 7 AM. People were still filing in—maybe 30 or 40 early arrivals. Ken Coleman made the anouncement: "Ladies and gentlemen, now batting for the Red Sox, number 9, Bill Nowlin." My name appeared in lights on the Diamond Vision screen.

I stepped into the box where The Kid had once stood. And Yaz. And Jim Rice, and way back when, Tris

Speaker and Babe Ruth. The Green Monster beckoned in the distance. Despite reports to the contrary, it looked miles away. Could I put one in the center field bleachers? Drive one off The Wall? Or even bounce one off the warning track?

No, it wasn't Bob Feller on the mound, nor Nolan Ryan, nor Bob Gibson in the 1967 Series. It was a pitching machine. The first pitch was a little high, the second, the same. I asked them to adjust it lower (had Ted ever made such a brash request of Rapid Robert?), and finally I just ticked a couple. One more adjustment to bring the pitch down, and finally I fouled one hard off the backstop. Then a one-hopper, also foul, into the left field seats. 3-2. (I'm leaving out a few others I missed completely.) Finally, one that might have been a single in a real game, if the second baseman had been shading towards first. And was a little slow. Strangely, there were no calls for me to emerge from the dugout to tip my cap to the fans.

cluded. As a result, the last major league franchise to integrate its lineup began to draw more African-Americans to the games, and cheers and jeers were now being shouted in Spanish as well as English. In 1998, when Pedro Martinez joined the Red Sox pitching staff, the Sox provided scores of tickets to Dominican organizations in the city and Dominican flags were proudly unfurled throughout the park. When Korea's Jin Ho Cho started a few games in midseason, there was a resultant increase in Asians or Asian-Americans at Fenway. Happily, Fenway crowds now better reflect the racial mix found outside the ballpark.

Sometime in the late 1970s, I upgraded from the Lansdowne Street bleacher ticket windows to the Yawkey Way gates, where you could buy reserved grandstand tickets. If you went by yourself and asked for a "single" you could often score some amazing seats, especially if you arrived an hour and a half before game time, when the ushers noisily hauled up the heavy corrugated iron doors to admit the ticket-buying public. Several times I got *the* seat, front row, center, immedi-

ately behind home plate. Occasionally, you could get rooftop box seats for a different sort of thrill, before they put up the luxury boxes.

I've seen a lot of great games at Fenway. There were times both in 1986 and in 1998 when it seemed the Red Sox would invariably stage a late inning comeback to snatch victory from the jaws of defeat, almost as if it were part of the game plan. More typically, however, were the seasons when

they would push two or three runs across in the ninth, but fall just short. There's always something about the ninth inning at Fenway Park.

I was there for Dave Morehead's 1965 no-hitter, the last one a Sox pitcher has thrown in the hitter-friendly confines. I was there for every one of the last four games of the 1967 Impossible Dream season, and was one of the first half dozen fans to rush out onto the field and clap Jim Lonborg on the back

If Boston's Fenway Park is demolished by wrecking balls sometime early in the 21st century, at least two or three other Fenway Parks will still live on for a while, thanks to the Red Sox, ballplayer Tim Naehring and, ironically, Bucky Dent.

"Fenway Park II" was built in February 1989 in Delray Beach, Florida, as part of the Bucky Dent Baseball School. It is a near-replica of Fenway Park, commemorating an event every Red Sox fan would like to forget: the surprise home run hit by Bucky Dent to win a one-game playoff which sent the Yankees to the World Series instead of the Red Sox back in 1978.

"Now it's not a mini Green Monster," says Larry Hoskin, GM of the Bucky Dent Baseball School. "It's the Green Monster! It's a major league-sized field. It's 315 feet from home plate. Our wall is 35 feet high—Fenway's is 37. The Wall is the same length. The scoreboard is painted the same size and it's frozen in time to the exact point when Bucky hit his home run. Same color. Same everything." [The Red Sox had been leading the game 2-0 after innings. The scoreboard depicts the temporary yellow "3" posted after Dent's home run, which pulled the Yankees ahead in the top of the 7th.]

"We have a net on top that's 15 feet wide, and goes back at a 45 degree angle, almost the same as Fenway. Now the rest of the park, the dimensions aren't the same because they didn't have the land and because the light poles were already there, but the Green Monster itself is the same dimensions, pretty much."

Tim Naehring, the very popular veteran infielder with the Boston Red Sox in the 1990s, has also built a replica of Fenway Park, this one in Miamitown, Ohio, not too far from his native Cincinnati.

Naehring says, "We basically built a 90% replica, so The Wall is 32 feet high and 200 feet long. We have the actual scoreboard on the Green Monster, it's a painted version of the 1975 World Series game. We have the Morse Code just like the real Fenway Park has. We basically did everything just like the real one is."

Tim Naehring has founded a non-profit organization called Athletes Reaching Out (ARO), and ARO plans a new replica facility in the Boston area. Mike Janedy, director of the Boston chapter, says "Tim wanted to build one in Boston because Boston was his second home. It will be in the quarries in Quincy. We're going to build a facility there. We've already got the architect—HOK out of Kansas City which the Red Sox are using—they built Camden Yards. They've been up here. They've seen the land, which is being donated. The Yawkey Foundation has already given $100,000 for startup costs. We're looking to raise about $4 million to build this. It's going to be a real enclosed field with dugouts and a Little Fenway museum, really a real facility We want to make sure the outside is done right. We'll have lights and the whole works. It will be 80-90% scale to the real Fenway.

"The only thing we'll do differently is that we'll leave the infield dirt. That way everybody can play on it—college, high school. We're basically going to leave it open for everybody to play for free. We'll do some things like softball leagues and still, where we'll get an entrance fee, but for the kids—high schools and Little Leagues—they're going to get it for free. We're going to try to get as many kids from around New England to come in and play."

"[Once the original Fenway Park is replaced] I think there's going to be incredible support base in Massachusetts for it, because it will be the only one that is there."

Well, maybe not. The Red Sox themselves jumped into the act in March 1999, with yet another field—a youth baseball facility to be built in Ramsay Park in the Roxbury section of Boston, less than a mile from Fenway Park. This one will be named after Red Sox star and current batting coach Jim Rice.

Funds for the design and construction of the new field will come from the Red Sox share of the proceeds from the 1999 All-Star Workout Day and Celebrity 21 Home Run Contest.

The Jim Rice Field at Ramsay Park will include a miniature version of Fenway Park's left field "Green Monster," as well as home and visitors dugouts, a backstop, bullpen, foul poles, lights, scoreboard, fencing bleacher seating, an irrigation and drainage system, public address system, restrooms, a concession stand and storage space.

It is quite a tribute to this beloved park, the original Fenway Park, to have so many replicas created in its image. If we lose the original Fenway Park, it seems there will be at least a few others—in Florida, Ohio and Massachusetts—to remind us a bit of that which once was.

Living at Fenway

There can be some very nice parks, and more comfortable ones. With the right touch, the right input and sensibilities, architects can come up with a very nice new home for the Red Sox—maybe even one which decades later will inspire feelings similar to the ones I feel for Fenway. However, unless they can figure a way to build off of the same footprint, it will no longer be the park where Babe Ruth played, and Tris Speaker and Ty Cobb and Ted Williams and Walter Johnson, or for that matter Nolan Ryan and Mark McGwire and Wade Boggs and Roger Clemens. It may be a wonderful place to watch baseball, as Camden Yards is, but it will lack the same spiritual aura that infuses every corner of today's Fenway Park.

in congratulations. My sister and I tore up and took home some blades of Fenway grass that day. I was there, sitting on the steps in section 17, to catch the perfect view of Fisk's Game 6 game-winning home run in the 1975 World Series. It took us going eight nights in a row, but a friend of mine and I were there when Yaz finally got his 3000th hit. I was there the night Roger Clemens threw his first 20-strikeout game, counting each whiff from the very first "K" in the first inning.

Unfortunately, I was also there for a certain game—the last one of 1978—which the three authors of this book have tried as hard as possible not to mention.

When my son Emmet was born, one of his first visits ever was to Fenway Park at age 6 weeks. His first game was September 4, 1991. The Red Sox won 2-0 that day. About six months later, he was baptized in a more orthodox church.

I haven't lost the enthusiasm—even the need—to *be* there. Once or twice during the winter, I just drive by, maybe browse the souvenirs at Twins Enterprises across the street. Just to pay a visit, just to be nearby. There can never be another Fenway Park.

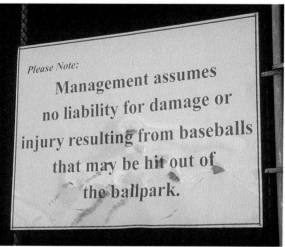

Please Note:
Management assumes no liability for damage or injury resulting from baseballs that may be hit out of the ballpark.

FENWAY SAVED

Everyone wants to save Fenway Park. Many would literally like to see the ballpark kept intact forever. Others, no less loyal to the legacy of Fenway, see its replacement as necessary to ensure the future of baseball in Boston. Both groups want the spirit of Fenway to live forever.

For all who have spent precious time there, it will be a sad day indeed when the wrecker's ball begins to knock down the brick facade, great metal jaws lifting out what they can grip and depositing it in the back of large trucks, while bulldozers push away all the rubble which is left. Memories, however, are not so easily disposed of.

Those who have enjoyed Red Sox baseball at Fenway Park will continue to savor those memories, even those that are impossible to articulate. This book, with numerous photographs of all aspects of the park and moving tributes from players and fans alike, will help us in this regard. Though the old park will eventually be no more, and the personal experiences we have all enjoyed may gradually begin to fade, we can continue to relive those moments through the pages of this book.